Sel...ng for Virgins

The Concept of
meta-morphose International

David Baker
&
Lucy Ryan

RYAK PRESS

First published in the United Kingdom
by Ryak Press in 2008

Ryak Press
Idsall House
Presbury
Gloucestershire
GL52 3AY

www.sellingforvirgins.com

ISBN 978-0-9560116-0-2

British Library Cataloguing in Publication Data
A catalogue record for this book is available from the
British Library.

Typeset by Edit Expert, www.editexpert.350.com

Printed in the United Kingdom

Contents

+ yes

ethical
undertake the
nature of the
....

1. In [?] I took the trouble to request a
review copy and read

bugo-drum

It's not a everche moment

— ves
trouble agas
enough talks
on whatever

there or for +
for between ...
..ls.

that a ..... It's given of tried flextua   approach/technique)
leads to proven   outlines with an easy to read manual.

Introduction

If at first you don't succeed, try and try + try again

Why This Book Is What You've Been Waiting For...

Anyone Can Sell

There's no such thing as a natural salesperson. We believe this book can teach *anyone* to sell, no matter what your current skills, experience or job title. We'll show you how to sell effectively and enjoyably, without clever tricks, arm-twisting or pushing customers through a sales process. By learning the simple techniques in this book, you can pick up the basics of selling within hours, even if you've never so much as made a cold call or offered a product to a customer – and better still, you'll enjoy selling and build relationships that generate business over and over again.

Are You a Sales Virgin?

There's no shame in being a sales virgin. If you've never sold anything in your life before, remember even the best salespeople had to start somewhere – including us! Maybe you've tried your hand at sales but weren't very successful, or simply hate the idea of being a 'pushy' salesperson. Well, we have good news for you. You've just hired not one but two of the UK's leading sales coaches, and neither of us believes 'pushing' customers to buy is an effective selling technique. We'll teach you the simplest and most effective secrets of selling, which are absolutely nothing to do with 'processing' customers or other dubious, unethical tactics. Within these pages you'll find unique and easy sales techniques used by top-performing sales stars all over Europe. These techniques

1

are so effective, we're hired by well-known businesses to share our knowledge with existing corporate sales teams. People trained in our methods win national sales awards and consistently outperform everyone around them. We've turned even the most 'unlikely' candidates into the brightest and best sellers of their generation, and we can do the same for you.

Why We Can Help You Sell

You're probably wondering who we are and why we believe we can help you sell. Well, we're the creative and practical minds behind sales training at meta-morphose – the organisation responsible for turning thousands of people into outstanding sales professionals. At meta-morphose, we teach graduates and corporate sales teams the fundamentals of sales success, and meta-trainees are hired by leading businesses all over the world.

meta-selling

We call the combination of sales theory and practice taught at meta-morphose the 'meta-selling technique', and we believe meta-selling is quite simply the most effective way to learn how to sell. Our techniques are totally ethical: meta-selling isn't about being cleverer than your buyers or manipulating people. Selling should never be about how many people you can pressure into buying your product. It's about relating honestly to customers and understanding their needs. We believe when a sale is completed, both customer and salesperson should walk away delighted.

Although anyone can learn meta-selling to improve their sales abilities, our methods are primarily for people who know very little about selling. As coaches at meta-morphose, we see a constant influx of bright people who have the desire to be great at selling, but little knowledge about the sales process. These people go on to become some of the best salespeople of their generation, yet when they come to us they're total sales virgins. So our techniques are designed to turn the novice into the supernova. We hope you're ready to be transformed...

DAVID: Before I founded meta-morphose, I worked as a consultant. My forte used to be rescue jobs - going into companies and getting salespeople out of bad habits. It was without a doubt the best way to find out which sales techniques and behaviours work and which don't. Every day, I saw real-life examples of failing sales teams and studied salespeople who weren't performing. I also studied the successful salespeople - the minority that carried the team.

After some years as a consultant, I was asked to advise an outfit in the West Midlands who resold fuel. What they offered was so specialist they hadn't had any competition before, and their salespeople thought it was a good day if they had one appointment - usually a lunch appointment. But now BP had decided to muscle in on the market and the company owners were terrified. They could literally fold overnight if their customers chose BP, which was a very real possibility. The country was also in recession and salespeople were being shed left, right and centre. The salespeople in this particular company were so set in their ways I didn't think I could do anything with them. So I struck upon a new idea. I persuaded the company to let me train a small selection of people, in what was effectively an early version of the meta-morphose method, and bring my trainees onto the sales team. I didn't know whether this would work - all I knew was if I selected people who had no previous sales training and were essentially a blank canvas, I could teach them the techniques I knew worked from scratch. Within 12 months my salespeople had achieved some staggering sales results for the company - even bringing sales from Europe. Suddenly my position went from 'consultant' to 'the man who makes businesses'! The company sold several years later for many times the value it had been when I was brought on board - and by then I had begun training meta-selling and offering trainees to other businesses. And meta-morphose was born...

We believe the meta-selling technique combines the most effective sales theory and practice available, so if you're new to sales you've just found the best training course you could hope for. If you're already in sales, we urge you to reconsider practices you may previously have been taught and try an ethical selling programme proven to work and work well. Our techniques aren't born from theory, but from hard evidence gained by training thousands of people and seeing them repeatedly enter the top 5% of their profession.

LUCY: I don't think I'm unusual in that I 'fell' into selling 20 years ago. It found me, rather than me seeking it out, as making 120 ad sales calls a day provided me with an income whilst I was on the stage. After a year I realised that I enjoyed it more than singing (at least it paid me!) and a sales career was born. Like many of you, I was expected to acquire the skills on the job. It wasn't until I went on my first sales training course five years after going into selling – and by then already managing a team of 12 people – that I got that great 'aha' moment: so that's how you do it! For the next 15 years I became obsessed with one question:

'What are the characteristics of successful salespeople?'

By the time I came to run the meta-morphose training centre 10 years later, where we were responsible for transforming up to 100 people a month into sales professionals, I had begun to form my own ideas. But working every month with a different group of bright, talented and dedicated young people from across Europe forced mere ideas into hard facts. By the time we'd guided the first 3,000 young people through their first year of selling, the behavioural patterns of success were evident time and time again. Even running my own sales consultancy in the last five years, when I've been privileged to work with highly experienced salespeople and sales leaders, the same behaviours are unmistakable. These behaviours are what we teach at meta-morphose and what you'll learn in this book, along with the straightforward selling framework that every successful salesperson uses – whether they're aware of it or not.

Ignore the Hype – This Is the 'How To'
This book is all about how to sell – and we promise it's easy and fun, just like the meta-morphose training courses. It isn't an instruction manual or a collection of dull sales philosophies that examine the ins and outs of the sales process without offering any real practical advice.

LUCY: This is unashamedly the book I've wanted throughout my sales career and couldn't find. A sales book for people in business or running their own business that looks beyond the hype of selling and into the how to. Because if you strip away the façade of selling, what you're left with is, in essence, remarkably simple. You offer your product, service or concept to a potential customer and help them decide whether or not it meets their needs. And it doesn't matter whether it happens face to face, over the phone or via the internet – the same simple process is taking place.

You'll learn by doing – just like trainees at meta-morphose – and we'll also share with you real-life examples from meta-morphose trainees who use the meta-selling techniques in the field. This book offers you simple instructions on how to sell, but we want you to laugh, think and more than anything see it our way – the meta-morphose way.

If you're new to selling (and even if you're not so new), we believe you need a 'how to' guide. There's no such thing as a natural salesperson. It really is unlikely you'll pick up sales by instinct alone, especially with all the contradictory and unethical material flying around. We certainly believe you should listen to your instincts when you're involved in sales, but without a basic selling framework you probably won't progress very quickly. Sales *is* simple – but only when you know how. As sales trainers we've spent years doing the trial and error for you, and we promise our way is the easiest, most enjoyable and most rewarding method out there.

Within these pages you'll find answers to the basic questions you've been longing to ask about sales. Questions like:

- What's the first thing I should say on a cold call to a customer?
- How do I find people who might want to buy from me?
- How do I ask for business without sounding desperate?

These are the sorts of questions experienced salespeople probably think have obvious answers, but that doesn't mean they have the right answers!

[handwritten margin note: More people (the author) understand that salespeople are their customer and they empathise with them]

Make This Book Your Own

How you read this book is entirely up to you. Dip in and out or read from front to back, back to front – it's your call. And it's not all about what your head tells you. Your heart and your instinct will let you know which parts of this journey are precisely the kind of route you want to follow – which parts *feel* exciting for you and *sound* interesting. Which turning you want to take, which avenues you want to explore and which areas look surprising. This isn't a manifesto that you have to follow word for word. This book is a framework on which you write your own rules.

What Will This Book Offer Me?

Given that hearsay states salespeople 'overpromise and underdeliver', we'll be careful with what we offer. But this is what we believe you'll get from this book:

- The confidence and the ability to sell – and even make your bank balance look a little healthier.
- A demystification of the sales process. This is shamelessly a how-to book, during which we'll be your sales coaches. We'll take you through the practical and professional

world of selling, and show you how to make selling natural and enjoyable for you and your customers.

- A down-to-earth approach with no jargon. Well, nearly. There are three acronyms, but we promise they're there for a reason!
- Other people's stories. The best learning comes from exploring and learning from other people's successes (and failures) so you can decide the path you want to take.
- The buyer's perspective. meta-selling is all about the buyer's point of view – you can't sell if there's no one to buy!
- A belief in you. We firmly believe that everyone can sell, whether you work for an organisation or run your own business. You just need the confidence, skills and desire.
- A positive and progressive look at the world of buying and selling – an understanding of what it's going to take for you to stand out from the crowd in the highly competitive world we operate in.

By the time you've finished this book, you'll be primed and raring to make your first sale. Are you ready to learn sales the meta-morphose way? Let's get started!

beginners' bible

Part I
Prepare Yourself for Some Fun

1

About the meta-morphose Method

Our Ethics: Helping Buyers to Buy

One of the first things we explain to trainees at meta-morphose is that selling isn't something you do to someone. It's about helping people to buy. To help someone to buy, you have to understand enough about what's going on in their heads, lives, worlds and business to actually find out if what you've got is of use to them or not. Selling is about being a sincere person and finding out if the buyer needs what you're offering. If a buyer faces several choices, as a good seller you should be able to present the competitive advantages of your product in a way that helps your client make a decision. And if you don't have what somebody needs at that point in time, you should save everybody time and walk away. Of course, you also have to understand that customers won't *necessarily* say 'Yes, I'll take it!' straight away. There's a difference between saying 'No' and saying 'No, I'm not sure. Will you help me see why this is right for me?' We'll talk more about that in Part II.

Why Ethical Selling Works

We firmly believe selling should be totally ethical every step of the way, from being honest about your purpose to talking frankly about what your products can and can't do. Not only is this simply the right way to behave, it's also the best way to excel at sales. Helping buyers to buy is an ethical way to sell, because if you see things from the buyer's point of view, it's very difficult to sell them something they don't need or to put them through an unpleasant process. It's not ethical to *sell* to people. Nobody likes being sold to. But people do like being helped to buy.

We've met and worked with many exceptional sales-people, and we can tell you categorically that the best sellers are simply genuine, nice people who want to talk about a product they see value in. We believe sales should never be about how many people you can make buy from you. Trying to coerce others into buying products may win a few customers in the short term (and we stress *may*), but it's not the strategy of excellent salespeople. Truly exceptional sellers are among the most reputable people you'll ever meet.

Part of what you'll learn in this book is the importance of making a connection with someone in order to build trust. Basically, until someone feels comfortable with you, it's very difficult to help them buy. You can't walk into a room not making eye contact, looking at the floor and not making any real connection with someone and then expect them to buy from you.

DAVID: I used to work with a guy called George, who was without a doubt one of the best salespeople I've ever met. He was brilliant, just brilliant. He always made a genuine connection with customers and never sold anyone anything they couldn't afford - at least not without an argument. If he thought a customer was spending too much money he'd say, 'Are you sure you can afford this?' Even if the customer was totally adamant they wanted to spend more on something bigger, George would make sure they were comfortable and happy doing so. He really was an extraordinary chap and a very good salesperson. We all instinctively like people who are trustworthy. The kinds of people who don't try to bullshit you or tell you what you want to hear. If you don't trust someone, surely the last thing you would do is listen to their recommendations about what you should buy?

Good salespeople are just nice people. They're trustworthy, and potential customers buy from them because they feel safe. Makes sense, doesn't it? And believe us, we've seen the proof that ethical salespeople get the best results. Not only with first sales, but also a major (and often forgotten) part of the sales process: repeat sales. If you're just after a few one-night stands, this book can help you achieve just that. But if you'd also like some long-term committed relationships with customers – relationships where you can win repeat business with very little effort – you've also come to the right place.

Learning the meta-morphose Way

meta-selling is about bringing out your natural sales personality – the likable, trustworthy and motivated person inside all of us who sells without even trying. We'll talk more about personality shortly. However, first we'd like to tell you the key ideas behind our training at meta-morphose and in this book. The first is this:

- Learn the basics
- Go over the basics
- Go over the basics again

On our training courses we lay down the basics, then go over them again and again. There isn't an advanced stage because selling is easy. As we go back over what you've learned, we fill in the gaps and answer questions, but the whole time the basic processes are learned again and again until they're second nature.

Get REPEC

Second, our training courses teach five simple stages of selling that will help you glide through the sales experience effortlessly and easily. When you go through them in the correct order, these stages will ensure you make the right moves when you sell, and don't get flustered or disorientated. The five stages are:

Rapport
Explore
Position
Expand
Commit

We have a handy acronym for these stages:

REPEC

You can think of REPEC as selling etiquette. It's more a set of guidelines than rules, and we encourage you to relax and get comfortable as you're working your way through them.

Whenever sales goes right, we can guarantee the seller – consciously or unconsciously – is moving through these stages, and this simple etiquette is the core of everything we teach at meta-morphose. You'll learn all about REPEC in Part II, but before you reach that section you need to find out about the fundamentals of meta-selling: how to see things from the buyer's point of view. This begins with learning about yourself, the buyer and your product, and we've got some great advice and exercises later on to help you do just that.

A Sordid Beginning

LUCY: At meta-morphose we've always given trainees a step-by-step guide to selling. But in the beginning, the five stages - rapport, explore, position, expand and commit - didn't have such nice, professional words or an acronym like REPEC to explain them. So David decided on a catchy collection of words to describe our guidelines: SEPEC. What does SEPEC stand for?

Stimulation
Exploration
Penetration
Examination
and (wait for it) Consummation

We tried out SEPEC during the meta-morphose training sessions, but unfortunately I couldn't keep a straight face while we were training it. Nor could the so-called adults we were training. So regrettably we scrapped all the stimulation and penetration and replaced them with plainer words that I could talk about without bursting out laughing. Sorry about that. However, whether you're penetrating or positioning, these five simple stages are central to your success as a salesperson. Yes, you have to be a nice person. Yes, you must be sincere. But you also need to know how to make your move, and in the case of sales this begins with five straightforward stages to guide you.

All about attitude

Attitude Is More Important than Aptitude

At meta-morphose, we firmly believe attitude is more important than aptitude. Your attitude to life is more important than any abilities people say you have or haven't got. So if you know nothing about sales, we promise you can learn to sell bigger and better than really experienced salespeople extraordinarily quickly, if you have the right attitude. Throughout this book, you'll be encouraged to feel good about yourself and what you can achieve regardless of aptitude or prior sales knowledge, because this will help you achieve a lot very quickly.

DAVID: I never had a particularly brilliant time at school, and in fact I remember my very first day – aged 5 – clinging to my mother's skirts and crying my eyes out because I didn't want to go. My memories of school and teachers are largely of being told what I couldn't do. I even had teachers telling me I'd never be good at anything – ever! Now I'm sure there are some really inspirational teachers out there. There must be. They can't all be awful. But there are a fair few who don't bother trying to instil kids with a good self-image and a healthy attitude to failure. In fact, far from encouraging kids to try again and not be beaten down

14

when they don't succeed, I remember teachers really giving me a hard time for failing. We put a healthy dose of antidote to previous education in meta-morphose training, and believe me: no matter what you've been told at school or anywhere else for that matter, you can be a brilliant salesperson if you have the right attitude.

Learn by Doing It

What's the last key ingredient of meta-selling? Learn by doing it. This is something we'll teach throughout this book, and doing it is essential for you to become a fantastic seller. A vital philosophy behind training at the meta-morphose school is that trainees learn through action. They take part in selling scenarios, give presentations and participate in all sorts of other activities designed to prime them for the sales environment. When we train face to face, it usually takes around a week to teach meta-selling and that week includes some highly unique and unusual methods. What are they? We won't tell you just yet – after all, we've only just got to know each other. But maybe you'll find out more later on...

In this book we've included a number of suggestions about doing it, or exercises, so you can recreate the meta-morphose training course at home. Don't be scared about doing it. We won't be asking you to throw off all your clothes just yet (at least, not in Part I). All we suggest is that a little bit of thinking and experimentation will reap big rewards. In fact, before we go on to talk about personality, let's get you doing it right now.

DOING IT: If we haven't convinced you how not to sell, try this out.

is sales sexy?

selling as sex!

Trying to reduce sales sexy.

sex sells

Next time you're in the pub, we dare you to ask someone you've never met before: 'Will you buy me a drink please?' Try to keep your voice as emotionless as possible. If the first person you ask says no, repeat the same sentence in exactly the same way to everyone in the pub. Will you get a drink? Maybe, maybe not. Will you enjoy asking strangers for something without building up any kind of relationship first? We doubt it.

If you don't fancy sounding like a robot, why not try being a sales Casanova. Simply approach someone you don't know, chat them up a bit, then drop into the conversation: 'I'll have a pint of lager please.'

Again, you may well get yourself a free drink. But how do you think people feel about being propositioned in this way? Used? Confused? After all, it's not usually the way people relate to each other. And how do you feel? Comfortable? Happy? Imagine doing this every time you go to the pub – not a nice prospect, is it?

Anyway, that's enough about meta-morphose and meta-selling for the moment. We hope we've convinced you we don't believe in leaving your integrity at the door to be a great seller, and that meta-selling isn't complicated or confusing. Now, let's talk about you...

2

Why Great Salespeople Have Great Personalities

At meta-morphose, we find people with excellent sales personalities and train them in meta-selling. When they've been trained, we place them in sales positions with companies all over the world. How do we find people with 'excellent sales personalities'? We look for four key character traits:

Motivation
Enthusiasm
Resilience
Likeability

Or as we call them: MERL. You may have already guessed motivation, enthusiasm and resilience are good personality traits for salespeople to have. But maybe you hadn't considered likeability as a key personality trait for potential sales trainees. Yes, that's right – likeability. We told you good salespeople are pleasant, considerate and thoughtful. Enthusiasm is also important. It doesn't matter if someone has qualifications coming out of their ears – if they can't get enthusiastic about selling, it will be difficult for them to get excited about their products and bring out desire in others. And of course, it's important to be resilient. Our trainees have to be able to take a knock or two without falling apart.

Why Your Personality Is Perfect for Sales

When we choose meta-morphose trainees, we're looking for people who already exhibit the MERL personality traits. But we believe MERL can be learned, or rather developed, for selling situations. As you move through this book, you'll be shown ways to bring out your own natural motivation, enthusiasm, resilience and likeability for sales. You won't find it difficult, because developing your MERL is mostly about being yourself and selling products you genuinely believe in.

Before we take on trainees at the meta-morphose training school, we put potential candidates through a group interview process to identify MERL. Candidates are observed playing a variety of role-playing games so we can find out which personality traits are most prominent. People who've already had sales experience often think they're in a better position than the sales virgins, but they're not. In fact, people with previous sales training are often less likely to exhibit high levels of MERL.

DAVID: Most of the people we choose to train at meta-morphose are in no way gregarious or loud, or have any of your 'typical' salesperson characteristics. In fact, we're much more likely to choose candidates who are thoughtful, curious and have a genuine interest in the people they talk to. Of course, we've met some real characters over the years. Wanting to be a salesperson often goes hand in hand with certain personality traits – but you'll learn more about that later.

Marie Ann is an account manager at meta-morphose and helps us interview potential trainees for our training school. She's met hundreds of aspiring salespeople – some who have

MERL by the bucket load, and others who… well, let's just say they're less MERL-vellous.

> MARIE ANN: I've recommended some really likeable and enthusiastic candidates for the meta-morphose training school, but I also help weed out people who don't fit our criteria. These are often people who've had previous sales training and picked up old-fashioned ideas about selling. I interviewed a brilliant character recently who came out with some wonderful clichés from the old school of selling. 'Never trust anyone' was one. 'There are no friends in sales' was another. He talked a lot and thought he could sell anything to anyone. He probably had no idea why we didn't choose him for training, but he was a great example of what we don't want. Overbearing, opinionated people aren't good sellers, although they almost always think otherwise!

Motivation Is Your Greatest Asset

Out of the four MERL characteristics, we believe motivation is the most important for really successful salespeople. Perhaps you thought, as a sales virgin, your reputation was your greatest asset. Wrong! Although you'll learn practical selling techniques during the course of this book, remember at all times your motivation to succeed is absolutely essential. Everyone has motivation – it's just a question of applying it to the right area. The fact you're reading this book shows a good deal of motivation and we applaud you for it. Keep it up! Later in the book you'll learn all sorts of ways to feel motivated about selling, and in Part III we'll give you hints and exercises to help you stay motivated.

You're MERL-vellous – Naturally!

We know you've got a great personality. After all, why else would you have chosen to learn selling the meta-morphose way? But did you also know you have a great sales personality too? We promise you have, even if you've never sold anything before in your life. In everyday life, we're naturally motivated, enthusiastic, resilient and likeable. We exhibit the key characteristics of MERL.

Imagine the following scenario.

Your friend needs to buy a new television, but he doesn't know much about the different sets available, prices or credit schemes. Luckily you do and you've agreed to accompany him on a shopping trip. You're motivated to help him, but it's not a struggle. You enjoy helping people because you're a likeable person. When you get to the store, you see lots of new innovations and designs and talk enthusiastically with your friend about the many models available. You know widescreen models offer a superior entertainment experience, and try to help your friend picture the wonderful evenings he could enjoy watching cinema-quality pictures in his own home. However, he scoffs at the idea, claiming for the same price he could go to the cinema once a week. Now, of course you're resilient enough not to take this personally. He has a perfect right to express his opinion. But you're not sure he has all the information he needs to make that judgement. You concede the widescreen models are expensive, but explain he'll get a far better-quality, more durable product for the extra investment. In the end, your friend decides on a credit scheme for a widescreen TV. You both walk away happy. He's been given good advice and bought something that's right for him. You've used your knowledge to help someone.

So if you've ever been in a similar situation (and we're sure you have), you've exhibited the personality traits of a great salesperson. It's just a question of bringing those qualities to a sales situation and developing your skills with people you don't already know.

Being a MERL-vellous salesperson really is easy. If you're already a genuine, honest person who would only sell products or services you have a belief in, you're halfway there. This book will help you bring out your natural MERL in sales situations, and there are lots of exercises designed to help you express the fantastic sales personality we know is inside you.

Why Instinct Matters

At meta-morphose, we believe in instinct. Good salespeople go with their gut, their first hunch, feeling, intuition – whatever you want to call it – when it comes to working out people and situations. In fact, believing in intuition is a vital part of a winning sales personality, and you should make it part of yours too if you want to succeed as a seller. Yes, you can learn a lot from us about selling, and yes, there are guidelines you should follow if you want to be a super-sexy seller. But you should also listen to your own instinct or intuition – the feelings you get when you speak to people, often before any logical thoughts have raced to the forefront.

How do good salespeople use their instincts when they meet buyers? We find they tend to get strong feelings the second they walk into a sales situation about the people they're meeting. They're not thinking anything 'logical' like: 'OK, this guy is wearing a grey suit so he's obviously quite conservative in his views.' Or: 'She's wearing a lot of make-up so appearance must be important to her.' They're simply *feeling* what's going on. And they listen to these feelings and flex their behaviour ever so slightly to match the different people they interact with. They're not doing it in a calculated or conscious way. In fact, it's more than likely they don't even realise they're doing it.

> DAVID: Gut feeling or instinct is underrated big time. The best sellers I meet always have fantastic instincts and experience very strong feelings almost immediately in sales situations. And they listen to their gut feeling. Your instinct can tell you what you want to know much faster than any superficial analysis of a person. Sellers with good instincts can walk into a room and pick up what's going on in a second. Lucy has great instincts, and if something has gone wrong in a sales situation I can guarantee she'll instinctively know exactly what it is.

Salespeople are sometimes so preoccupied with *how* to sell, they forget to relate normally and naturally to people and to allow their natural instincts to come into play.

Developing Your Instincts
Have a think about your good friends and family members. Do you usually know the second you talk to them their mood or state of mind?

> DAVID: When I'm on the phone to one of my kids, I know immediately if they're unhappy. Within seconds. With people we know very well, we rarely question our instincts. We know we're right. Good salespeople experience something similar with buyers and most importantly they listen to that information.

22

Whether you realise it or not, you have great instincts. And you almost certainly already experience a strong sense of people's likes, values and attitude to life when you first meet them. It's just a question of acknowledging and listening to those feelings and adapting your behaviour to suit different people so you understand each other. If you're thinking that sounds a little bit insincere, think about the people you communicate with every day. Do you speak in exactly the same way with each of them? The way you talk to the landlord of your local pub is likely to be entirely different to the way you chat to your grandma. That doesn't mean you're being fake or false. It means you're a good communicator.

DAVID: One of the ways I help salespeople pay more attention to their instincts is to talk about a sales situation after it's happened, and ask the seller to relive it right down to the smallest detail. If we're talking about a face-to-face situation, I ask the seller to remember every visual detail they can - even how the walls were decorated, what kind of outfit the buyer was wearing, really every little thing. Then we go over what the seller feels about the situation. It doesn't matter what was actually said - what do they feel was happening? Did they feel the client was happy? Indifferent? Are they likely to have another supplier? When we go over a situation in this way, it's amazing the amount of information that was missed first time around because the seller wasn't listening to their instincts. It's easily done if you're new to sales and so caught up in getting everything right you forget to go with your gut feeling. By recreating the selling situation, we get a second opportunity to listen to the instincts we should have heard the first time. Once sellers learn to listen when they're actually in a sales situation, that's when they really start to do well. Incidentally, you'll learn how to try the after-sales analysis technique for yourself in Part III. It's amazing how effective it is!

So how can you learn to listen to your instincts when you're selling? Well, first of all you need to get really comfortable with knowing your product, seeing things from the buyer's point of view and the REPEC stages of selling. You need to learn about the parts of the sales process until they're second nature, and *practise* selling, even if you're just asking friends and family to carry out role playing with you. That way, when you come into a selling situation you'll feel relaxed, happy and able to let your intuitive voice talk to you. You also need to trust your own feelings when it comes to selling and *not to judge* people on preconceived notions of character. If in doubt, listen to your inner voice!

DOING IT: Here are two simple ways to practise getting in touch with your instincts.

Take deep breaths and concentrate on the sound and rhythm of your breathing. When you're relaxed, you calm down the hundreds of logical voices fighting for attention and allow your intuitive thoughts to reach the surface. Now try to guess something simple you don't know the answer to, like what the weather will be like for the rest of the day. If you're not right first time, don't worry. Just try again tomorrow. We believe in you. Just keep practising and we know you'll get there.

Try waking up at the weekend without setting your alarm. As soon as you wake up, guess what the time is in hours and minutes. If you haven't tried this before, you'll be amazed how accurate you are. When you've

just woken up, you're naturally very relaxed and likely to be more in touch with your intuition.

Now we've had a look at your personality and talked you through the meta-morphose way of doing things, it's time to play some mind games. You're going to learn some of the psychological reasons for people buying things, and the various stages we all go through when we buy a product. In short, you're going to get inside your buyers' heads and take a look around.

3

I'll Take It! Learning Why We Buy

Why do people buy? What motivates them to make a purchase, and what feelings and ideas are behind these motivations? We won't be going in for an awful lot of psychology in this book, but we do have some ideas about what drives and motivates us all when it comes to buying. Learning why we buy will help you relate to buyers and of course help them to make a purchase. Remember that you're a buyer too, so part of this learning process should involve having a think about yourself and what motivates you. Don't worry – we won't be asking you to lie down on a couch and tell us how you feel about your mother. But this chapter will help you realise we're all pretty similar when it comes to our motivations for buying. David has loads to tell you about our motivations as human beings and what this means when it comes to sales, so we're going to hand over to him for the rest of the chapter.

The Two Key Motivators:
Recognition and Acceptance

When we teach trainees at meta-morphose why we buy, we always start by showing them Maslow's Hierarchy of Human Needs. Maslow was a psychologist from the 1950s, and his theories about what motivates us are very well known. Maslow listed five different human needs and piled them up in a pyramid to show we're all motivated by similar things in a similar order, but some needs must come before others. The pyramid looks like this:

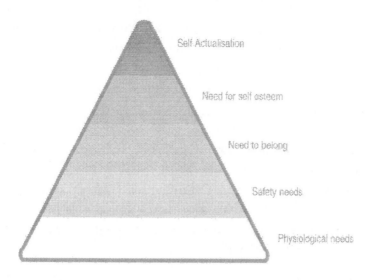

Self Actualisation

Need for self esteem

Need to belong

Safety needs

Physiological needs

You can see at the bottom of the pyramid are our physiological needs. These include eating, sleeping and other physical requirements. When our basic physiological needs are met, we move up to the next level of motivation – craving a safe environment. If our environment is safe, we're motivated to belong and so on up the pyramid until we come to self-actualisation: the need to broaden our minds and grow intellectually.

I'm sure you remember a time when you've been really hungry. That's a physiological need. According to Maslow, once your hunger has been taken care of you might consider finding out how your food is prepared, what all your friends are eating, whether the dish you're choosing shows off your culinary knowledge and finally whether it educates you in a new style of cooking.

I used to study psychology at university years ago, and Maslow was around then. If you've ever studied psychology at any level you've probably come across him. The reason his ideas are taught so often is because he was one of the few psychologists to study what motivates us as human beings, and of course our motivations are very important when it comes to sales. Actually, when Lucy was studying for her MSc in Positive Psychology, Maslow was still being referred to – almost 60 years after his original ideas were written!

I think Maslow was right about at least one thing – we do all need to meet our basic survival needs before we start thinking about anything else. If you were hungry or tired at the moment, I very much doubt you'd be reading this book. Was he right about everything else? I don't know. But at meta-morphose we have our own hierarchy of needs which we believe is more accurate, especially when we're thinking about sales. It looks like this:

You'll see the meta-morphose pyramid starts with survival needs, just like Maslow, but after that our ideas about human motivation are very different – and much simpler. After we've taken care of eating, sleeping and so forth, we have social needs to think about. The primary human social needs are acceptance and recognition, and we're all motivated to achieve these. All of us. I've never met anyone who wasn't driven by acceptance or recognition, and I don't believe anyone who says they aren't.

But I Don't Need Anyone!

You'll often hear people say they don't care what people think about them. I used to know a woman who spent a fortune on designer clothes and she always looked fantastic. I don't think I ever saw her in the same outfit twice. And she insisted that she didn't care what anyone thought of her. She claimed everything she wore was purely for herself and to make herself feel good. Rather foolishly, I suggested this couldn't be the case. 'You must care what people think of you,' I insisted. 'You can't tell me you're spending all that money on clothes not to be recognised by others. Unless you've got a room full of mirrors at home and you spend your whole time standing around in front of them.' Needless to say, I wasn't thanked for expressing those sentiments. In fact, she told me rather forcefully that she really didn't give a damn what anyone thought of her. But the truth is, she was looking for recognition just like the rest of us. She was looking to be recognised as a totally independent person who didn't need the approval of others.

Even people who're adamant that they don't need anyone's approval are motivated by a need to be recognised for this character trait. 'I don't care what anyone thinks!' they'll shout. 'Are you watching?' they're really saying. You'll find even people who live alone and rarely interact with others will have a cat they talk to, or some sort of TV personality they idolise. Or perhaps they'll have God syndrome and think they're being constantly watched and judged. However we express it, we all need acceptance or recognition. It's just part of our make-up as human beings.

Accept Me!

So our first basic emotional need is to be accepted by at least one other person. Someone else in the world has to think we're alright and approve of us.

Remember I was telling you about my first day at school and how I was in tears at the school gates clinging to my mother's skirts? She was pushing me through the railings gate, but the playground didn't seem like a very good place to be. It was full of kids running around, all dressed the same, and it looked to me like an emotional pit of terror. While I was blubbing and clinging to my mother, a teacher came over with another child – I've completely forgotten who he was now – and said, 'David, this is so and so. Come on, he'll show you around.' I remember the kid held his hand out, and although I was probably still blubbing I took it and went into the playground. I felt accepted by someone. The school play-ground didn't feel half as bad. Well, that's acceptance. It's a very basic and powerful human requirement.

We all need at least one person to approve of us, and for some people this is enough. They don't need anything else to meet their emotional needs. However, in our culture we tend to find acceptance relatively easily, and most people move up the pyramid at one time or another and begin to need recognition.

Adore Me!

After we've been accepted, we want to be recognised. In our culture this tends to happen no matter what background people come from. This is where the pyramid starts to narrow. Some of us want more than others. We want to be better and we strive for adoration.

In our training room at meta-morphose we have a picture of the most glorious lizard. It's a beautiful, multi-coloured animal with a red tongue sticking out of a silvery mouth. Under the lizard, there's a caption which says:

'Some people are different.'

This is a great metaphor for our need for recognition. Incidentally, salespeople often have an extraordinary need to be recognised. The need for recognition is often what drives them to take the emotional knocks and rejections that are often part of selling. At our training days we see some real fashion victims. Sometimes as part of the assessment we'll ask the really outlandishly dressed ones about what they're wearing. After all, meta-morphose trainees have to be resilient and able to take criticism if they're going to be successful. And they'll say to us, 'Yes, I know it's a bit over the top.' We're too kind to say, 'You just wanted to stand out and be recognised, didn't you?'

You'll find in almost all cultures people seek recognition and this can be expressed in all sorts of weird and wonderful ways. Have a think about the different ways people live all over the world and you'll identify all sorts of customs that are to do with being recognised socially. From the Amazonian tribes who stick discs of varying sizes in their lips to the pin-striped suits of big cities, human beings develop multiple ways of achieving recognition after their basic physiological needs are met.

Dollars, Pounds or Sex Appeal: What's Your Currency?

So how do we seek to be recognised? We're all different, so as you might expect we all have different ideas about what we want to be recognised for. We have different values, or as we call them at meta-morphose, currencies. We don't mean the pocket full of euros and dollars you might have left over from your last holiday. At meta-morphose, when we talk about currencies we mean the unique things each of us sees value in and wants to be recognised for. These can be any number of things, from a desire to be recognised as sensible and reliable, to valuing being self-sufficient or a go-getter. We all operate with a mixture of many different currencies and these are unique to the individual.

Let me give you an example. I love cooking. Making food for myself is OK, but what I really love is to cook for other people. There's no greater compliment than when people wipe their plates clean and ask for seconds. By doing so, they're recognising my culinary talents and cooking abilities. Being recognised as a great cook is one of my currencies. It really taps into something I value, and it's a true ego boost for me. It makes all the hours in the kitchen worthwhile. I've got loads more currencies though – just like all of us.

There are really hundreds of currencies, but very broadly speaking they fall into four categories:

- Possessions (cars, houses, companies)
- Power (knowledge and skill)
- Superiority (fitter, smarter, beautiful)
- Altruism (kind, generous, charitable)

When we take on graduates to learn meta-selling, it's fascinating to watch people lay their currencies on the table, so to speak, during our training courses. I can guarantee that there'll be at least one joker: someone who values making people laugh. If there are two jokers, I know we're in for a great week because they'll compete with each other and get funnier and funnier. They'll also respect and value each other too, because they're trading in the same currency. Another currency we always see at our training sessions is the 'sensible' currency. We see this played out over and over again with our graduates. Someone will really value being recognised as the sensible one, and they're usually automatically elected as group leader.

> **DOING IT:** Choose five people you know very well and work out their currency. What do they want to be recognised for and how do they go about gaining this recognition?

How Currency Will Help You Sell

Understanding people's currencies will help you develop essential trust and rapport with potential buyers, and can make the difference between being a good seller and a great seller (and it will also help you understand how people use what they buy to be recognised). Recognising your buyer's currency is one of the first steps in gaining their trust and building a bond. We all tend to trust and like people we feel are a little like us, or at the very least understand and don't directly contradict our values. As we've said before, good sellers bend and flex themselves ever so slightly to meet their buyer's personality. To be a good seller you have to become a *little bit* like your buyer.

This doesn't mean you have to pretend to share the currency of the person you're selling to. But it does mean it's very important to understand their currency and not trample on it. In other words, it's vital not to *devalue* the currency of people you're selling to. If you want to interest someone in what you have to offer, the second you devalue their currency you're on a fast road to nowhere. There's no way you can develop rapport if you've belittled the currency of the person you're selling to.

With people you know well, you probably already have an awareness of their currencies and are careful not to talk down what they see value in (or if you do, you're fully aware that you're doing it!). But if you've only just met a buyer, it can be a little more difficult to work out exactly what currencies they're trading in. So how do you work out currency in people you don't know very well? As with every part of the selling process, you should remember to listen to your instinct when it comes to figuring out your buyer. But on a more superficial level, there are often visual clues as to what currency your buyer is trading in. We call these clues trophies, and they can provide valuable insights into your buyer's personality.

The Trophy Cabinet

When people are looking to be recognised for something, they often surround themselves with all sorts of clues to let you know exactly what they value. These clues are what we at meta-morphose refer to as trophies. They're the objects that, on the surface at least, may help us work out what currencies our buyers are trading in. Trophies can be all sorts of things: a sports car, a photograph of someone with a celebrity – even a cabinet full of real trophies with engraved name plates. They're basically things people have around them to show others what they want to be recognised for.

Let's imagine you're in the office of a potential buyer. On the wall he has a picture of himself with Tiger Woods. You should feel pretty certain that this is a trophy. It's very unlikely anyone would put something like this up on the wall and expect people to ignore it. This person wants you to look at his picture, and hopefully comment on it. Recognise me, he's saying. Now, he may talk down such a trophy if you ask him about it. He may write it off as simply a great day out when he happened to meet a famous golfer. But he hasn't put it on the wall for you *not* to notice it. He wants you to say 'wow' – or at least *think* wow. And ideally he wants you to recognise what this trophy means: in this case, he almost certainly values being an accomplished golf player and would probably like to be very good at the game himself.

I personally don't like golf at all. But if I were to look at that picture of my buyer with Tiger Woods and say something like 'Isn't golf a big waste of time?' I'd instantly dissolve any rapport we'd built up between the two of us, probably permanently, because I'd be devaluing something my buyer clearly holds in high esteem. So it can be very important to work out people's currencies in a selling situation, and to look out for any trophies that may indicate what these currencies might be.

Flattery Gets You Nowhere

Have you ever heard the saying 'Flattery gets you nowhere'? In sales that's true too. Just because you've spotted someone's trophy, that doesn't mean it's a good idea to tell them in glowing terms how fantastic it is. Aside from the fact it would be very insincere behaviour (unless you really love Tiger Woods, of course), your positive responses to a buyer's trophies are unlikely to be appreciated. Yes, it's a good idea to understand the things your buyer values. But simply to flatter a buyer and tell them how wonderful their car is, or their designer suit or whatever trophy they're waving around, doesn't really work. Why? Because as a salesperson it's likely your recognition doesn't have much value for a buyer. The recognition that really has value is from someone we look up to and want to emulate. And I'm afraid to say, in a sales situation that's unlikely to be you.

Once you understand the idea of trophies, you'll start noticing them everywhere. For some people, the contents of their supermarket trolley are trophies. You'll see when friends stop to talk to each other, they'll sometimes check out the contents of each other's trolleys. And you might even see people arranging their trolleys to display the things they want to be recognised for at the top, and hide the things they really *don't* want to be recognised for at the bottom. Of course, one person's pile of trophies could be another person's meaningless trolley full of shopping. Some people might claim they'd never be as shallow as to care about what's in their shopping basket. But they're simply trading in a different currency. They have different values and different trophies. For them, a shelf full of books might be the objects they present to the world to gain recognition.

> DOING IT: Work out one of your own currencies.
> What do you do, or buy or take part in that you hope to
> be recognised for? What do you do to stand out from
> the crowd, and what are you trying to tell people about
> yourself? Now figure out the trophies you spread around
> yourself to demonstrate that currency. It could be one
> thing or ten things, but trophies are always objects that
> have a real emotional charge: something you love people
> to look at.

If there are hundreds of different currencies, then there are probably hundreds of thousands of different trophies. We can't tell you how to spot people's trophies in a selling situation. You have to go with your instincts and your natural abilities to work out what's going on. But being aware of the trophies people surround themselves with and the many currencies we all use can help you enormously when it comes to working out what a buyer is all about, and developing essential trust and rapport.

4

How to Read a Buyer's Mind

Now David has talked a little about the psychology behind buying, it's time to take mind reading to the next level. We're going to look at exactly how buyers think when they're considering making a purchase. If you feel this sounds a bit intimate, you're right. It's important to get close and understand as much as possible about how buyers think before you take the plunge and start selling.

Sellers sometimes think they need to lead buyers through a sale. But this is wrong. We should never forget buyers have an awareness of the market, their own ideas about the products they need and a good deal of free will when it comes to making decisions. Our role is to *guide* them through a sale, offer them information and generally help in any way we can. To do this, we have to understand the different stages a buyer might go through before they buy.

LUCY: As a seller, it's really easy to get wrapped up in what we're doing and forget that buyers have an agenda of their own. They're not guided by our sales process - in fact, it's unlikely most buyers even know anything about the stages we follow as sellers. Buyers follow their own path, and they quite rightly get frustrated with sellers who don't understand or respect this.

What Buyers *Really* Think – the Buying Sequence

There are five stages buyers go through before they commit to buy something. At meta-morphose, we call these buyer stages 'PRIMED', and once you know them you'll be primed and ready to sell. We use a snazzy diagram to show the five stages buyers go through before making a buying decision:

We're going to take you through these stages one at a time, and while we do so you should have a think about how you make decisions when *you're* a buyer.

1. Present Reality – the Comfort Zone

This is stage one of the buying process, and in this stage it could be that a buyer is quite comfortable and not actively looking to change anything. They might be thinking about how their company is doing things at the moment and whether everything is happening as it should. They could have an idea that they'd like to change something, but aren't yet certain whether it's necessary.

2. Issues – Do We Have a Problem Here?

In stage two, your buyer may be experiencing some problems with how things are working at the moment, and they're assessing just how big these problems are. They're thinking about how exactly these problems are affecting the business at present and how urgent it is to make a change.

3. Future Map – the Dream Relationship

Buyers aren't stupid. Not only can they work out for themselves if their problem is big enough to warrant a change, they also often have an idea of what a great solution looks like. They may well have pictures in their head of exactly what would work for them before they go about looking for it.

4. Evaluation – Weighing Up the Pros and Cons

Next, the buyer weighs everything up. They think through the choices in front of them, and consider how they might choose a new supplier and what they'll gain as a result.

5. Decision – Shall We Make a Commitment?

In the decision-making stage, a buyer thinks about when they should make the decision whether to buy or not, who should be consulted about the final decision and what budget might be involved.

Moving Through the Stages

For someone to decide they want to buy from you, they've got to want to move from where they are now into a future stage. A buyer could be at any one of the PRIMED stages when they're approached by a seller, so as a salesperson it's important to be aware of the stages and of course to find out which stage a buyer is at. Why would a buyer want to move out of their existing stage and want to buy from you? Generally, because they've got issues with what they have already. As a salesperson, it's your job to find out these issues and help your buyer see how what you're offering can solve them. We'll talk more about finding out the stage your buyer is in and selling for each stage in Part II.

LUCY: Buyers do have a good idea of what they need and commonly they've done their research. They don't always know what is going on in the marketplace as well as you do and that's what they rely on you for. But your product or service isn't always going to be the right solution for them.

Walking in a Buyer's Shoes (Without Getting Blisters)

In order to really understand your buyers, it's important to walk in their shoes. When we see excellent sellers at work, all they're really doing is thinking about their customer and seeing things from their point of view. Walking with a buyer isn't painful. It's just a matter of understanding the stages they go through and following them, instead of dragging them through your sales process.

LUCY: When we train at meta-morphose, we tell our trainees that the buying process is like a road and we're literally walking with people down the road. Each stage a buyer passes is like a signpost, and at each signpost we're asking: 'How does it look for you here?' 'What are *the gaps you need to fill or the issues you need to solve?' 'What choices do you have and how are you going to make a decision?'*

We know you've bought things before, but we bet you've never really analysed the decision process you went through when you did. So now is your chance. We'd like you to think like a buyer so you can really understand their point of view. Imagine it's Saturday night and you're sat at home. You've got to decide what you're going to do with your evening and you're going to go through the five decision-making stages to get there, just as you would if you were a buyer.

Present Reality – Stuck on the Sofa
You're at home on the sofa watching a film. You check the time and realise it's 8 p.m. – time to have a think about your plans for the evening. Should you stay in and watch the film? You're only really watching it because it happened to be on TV, and you're beginning to wonder if there might be better movies to watch.

Issues – This Film Is Rubbish!
The film isn't very good and you're a bit bored. If you stay in you'll have wasted a whole evening watching a very average film, and there are loads of good films you really want to see. You decide you *would* prefer to watch a better film if you had the choice, but is this a big enough problem for you to change anything?

Future Map – I Know a Brilliant Movie
You know there are a few great films around at the moment and you imagine how much more enjoyable it would be to watch those instead. You check your pockets and find a £20

note, so you know you've got the cash to pay for a cinema ticket or a film rental.

Evaluation – Cinema, DVD or Something Else?

You think about the different ways you could find out about the films around at the moment. Film guides, the internet, the local newspaper... there are all sorts of resources you could use. You also think about whether you'd like to go to the cinema, rent a DVD or even buy a movie to watch at home.

Decision – Maybe This Film Isn't So Bad...

You have to make a decision quite quickly, since it's already 8 p.m. and the evening is slipping away. How long will it take to walk to the cinema as opposed to the DVD rental shop? What are the different costs of each alternative? In the end, you decide to stay at home. Thinking about all the different options without any guidance is just too time consuming and it seems easier to stay put. If you had a date to persuade you to choose one of the options, it might be a different story...

Hopefully this little flight of fancy helps you put yourself in a buyer's shoes, think about the decisions they go through and remember that people have ideas of their own before a seller comes along. We can't stress enough how important it is to see things from the buyer's point of view. But now let's get back to you and what you have to offer. You should be excited by now – you're only a few chapters away from getting into the sales process and losing your virginity.

5

What Do You Have to Offer?

Now you've got inside your buyer's head, you need to prepare yourself. It's time to get dressed up, focused and ready before you learn how to sell for real. Sound a bit contrived? Perhaps preparation does ruin the spontaneity of things a little bit. But we guarantee you a much better sales experience if you prepare and focus beforehand. In fact, not only will your selling be incredibly sexy, you'll save hours of naïve fumbling and help ensure your buyer has a fantastic sales experience. How should you prepare yourself before you start selling? Simple:

- Fall in love with your product
- Become intimate with your buyer's business

How to Love Your Product

At meta-morphose, we believe you have to fall in love with whatever you're selling before you can lose your sales virginity. Old-fashioned? Perhaps. But how can you sell something you don't like or respect? It's certainly not an ethical way to behave, and we don't believe you'll be a very convincing or enthusiastic salesperson if you do so. Having love for your products is a key part of meta-selling. Why? It ensures you're genuine and sincere when you sell – which is a fundamental ingredient of sales success. Without a genuine enthusiasm for your product you won't be an exceptional seller.

Falling in Love

How do you fall in love with your product? First of all, you should get to know what you're selling and learn everything you can about it. If you run your own business or want to sell things you create yourself, chances are you already know your products very well. We certainly hope so, anyway. However, if you're selling someone else's products you need to really get into bed with them.

- Find out how your product is made or produced and talk to the people who make this happen.
- Talk to people who use your product and find out how it works for them.
- Research your product's history on the internet, and find out everything you can about its origins and how it evolved for today's market.

Find out all you can and make really certain this product is something you can entertain a long-term sales relationship with. Get to know it inside and out. We should point out here that there's a difference between *knowing* your product and *loving* your product. You can know your product backwards, forwards and from all sorts of interesting angles *and* be able to list all its advantages, but you have to love what you're selling in order to be an exceptional seller. If after the 'getting to know you' bit the product or service isn't something you see value in, don't sell it. It's as simple as that.

But I Don't Know What I'm Selling Yet!

LUCY: If you don't know what you're selling and what it does for the customer, find out! You need to know why someone should buy from you and why they should choose your product over a competitor's. You should know what's great about what you're selling and, ideally, what's unique about it. If you don't see value in what you're offering, then you'll have a hard time persuading someone to buy it from you.

If you really can't find out what you're selling just yet, choose a product you like and use that for the time being. But bear in mind you really should go back over this chapter and try out the exercises with whatever it is you'll be selling eventually.

The Three-Way Mirror

Have you fallen in love yet? That's great, but loving your product isn't enough. You also need to be able to see it from your buyer's point of view. Why? So you can present it effectively and be honest about any disadvantages inherent in what you're selling. It also helps you learn what might appeal to buyers, so you can explain this without them having to work it out for themselves. You should do as much work as possible so you can save your buyers the trouble.

You need to view what you're selling from every angle, so you know everything looks great to a buyer before you launch into the sales process. If you were going out on a date, you'd probably have a look at yourself in the mirror before you left the house. You'd take a little time sizing yourself up and maybe straightening or adjusting things (we won't ask what) – it's exactly the same with selling. So let's give what you're selling a good looking over.

Your Best Side: Product Benefits

Everyone enjoys this bit. It's time to think about your best side: the fantastic benefits of what you're selling.

> **DOING IT: List ten positive things about your product or service, right now:**
>
> 1
>
> 2
>
> 3
>
> 4
>
> 5
>
> 6
>
> 7
>
> 8
>
> 9
>
> 10

Now we need to work out what your product attributes will do for buyers. So let's get them dressed up and presentable by turning them into product benefits. How do we do that? Easy. We take our attribute and add this simple phrase:

'which means that...'

Here's an example: 'Our printers now offer a digital printing service, which means that we can print material faster and at a lower cost.'

Let's try that with the positive things you've listed about what you're selling:

1

2

3

4

5

6

7

8

9

10

DAVID: When you're thinking about what you're selling from a buyer's point of view, it's important to remember your buyer isn't seeing what you're selling in its raw form. They're seeing an idealised version of themselves using your product or service, and they'll more than likely be considering just how that picture makes them appear to other people. So remember to help them see just *how your product will allow them to be recognised by others in a positive light.*

The Famous Five

You might also find it helpful to think about what you're selling alongside some famous buyer benefits used by marketers to promote products. Advertisers all over the world consider five buying benefits before designing TV, print and internet commercials.

These benefits are:

Status

Some products claim to offer self-esteem and a better image for the buyer. Advertisers suggest these sorts of products will make us look better, achieve success, appear affluent or generally improve our appearance to others.

Security

When we talk about security as a benefit, we're not thinking about burglar alarms. Products we feel are reliable and dependable, such as those with familiar brand names, appeal to our desire for security because we feel they're safe and we won't experience any nasty surprises.

Relationship with seller

Sometimes we know the products or services we use aren't the best available, but we continue to purchase them because we have a good relationship with the seller.

Value for money

Self-explanatory, this one. When we think we're getting a great financial deal, a product becomes very appealing. You see it everywhere: 'price lowered', 'great value', 'special offer', 'half price' and so on.

Habit

Products we've bought a hundred times before and have a set buying routine for appeal to our habitual instincts, or our appreciation of an easy, uncomplicated life.

> DOING IT: Imagine you're off on a date with someone. Don't worry, you don't actually have to do this one – unless you fancy it, of course. But we would like you to choose the venue. You have a choice of five:
>
> A cheap bar serving two-for-one drinks all evening.
> A very average pub you've been to loads of times before.
> A chain pub with predictable drinks and prices.
> An expensive cocktail lounge frequented by celebrities.
> An over-priced pub where your best mate works.
>
> Can you work out which venue appeals to which of the famous five buying benefits? It shouldn't be too difficult, but then we told you selling was easy. In fact, it's so easy we're not going to tell you the answers. You'll just have to trust your own judgement on this one.

When we enter into a relationship with a product, we're always looking for one of these benefits. They're known as the 'primary benefits' and they're sometimes given different names and identities. But whether you choose to call benefit one status or ego or benefit five habit or convenience, every successful product will satisfy one of these consumer desires. You can bet what you're selling will appeal to one of these desires too.

DOING IT: Next time you're watching commercials on TV, grab a pen and try to work out which of the five motivators each advert is trying to appeal to. Now have a think about what you're selling. Of the five benefits, which one best describes the buyer appeal of your product? You may find what you're selling offers more than one of these benefits, but it's likely to suit one more than all the others. Which one?

Your Not-so-best Side: The Disadvantages of Your Product

Love isn't perfect. Your product probably has disadvantages. But before we look at disadvantages that can't be solved, you should ask yourself: 'Is my product or service as good as it could be, or should it be improved before selling takes place?' Be honest with yourself here, because if there are problems with your product that *can* be ironed out then they *should* be ironed out. If you're selling something that's been sold by others before, ask the sellers if there are any improvements you think could and should be made. Then talk to the relevant people and get the improvements.

Now let's talk about disadvantages that can't be helped. Don't feel self-conscious about this: disadvantages exist in almost every product or service – at the very least for some customers some of the time. That doesn't mean your product isn't ready to sell. It just means before you start selling, you need to learn about these potential flaws so you can give potential buyers an honest and open appraisal of what they're getting for their money. If you're going to be ethical and honest, remember you're not looking for one-night stands. You're establishing committed relationships with your buyers, and you're hoping for future business and word-of-mouth sales that come with a good reputation for selling honestly.

> DOING IT: List five **disadvantages of your product here,** right now:
> 1
> 2
> 3
> 4
> 5

We hope that wasn't too painful. And at least they're out in the open now. You'll be using these notes later on when you're learning REPEC, and finding out in great detail how to deal with criticism and objection while you're selling.

The Rear-View Mirror: The Competition

Unless you're selling something totally unique, you're almost certainly going to have some competitors. People are always likely to offer similar products or services, possibly at a lower price. So you need to have a good look at what else is on offer. Otherwise, you'll find it difficult to have an informed conversation with buyers when they ask you why they should choose your product over another. The idea of competitors maybe sounds a bit intimidating, but we don't want you to worry. As long as you genuinely like what you're selling and communicate honestly, you needn't fear competition. Sometimes sellers feel they have to disguise from customers the fact there are similar products on the market. But your buyer will almost certainly have had a good look at what's on offer. You really need to find out just what else is out there so you're in the best position to inform and advise buyers, and present your product in the best possible light. There's no point telling customers all about the brilliant prices you offer if someone else is offering something similar at half your rates. Better to explain exactly the value buyers will get from your reasonably priced service.

> **DOING IT:** It's time to get to know the competition. Find three competitors and for each one write down an advantage their service has over yours:

Now we'd like you to tell us exactly how and why your product is better than all three of your competitors. This could be for a combination of reasons. Perhaps you offer a faster service at a lower price than two of your competitors, and a lower price for the same service as another. What makes your product unique or special? What's your favourite thing about the product you're selling? What makes it better than the rest? If you don't know, maybe you should be selling your competitors' products instead!

> LUCY: You should be able to differentiate your product, and know exactly how it is different and what this means for customers. So if you ring a company and someone says: 'I already use one of your competitors', you

can say: 'Great! But can I explain exactly what we offer that's different?'

Be Passionate: Create Product Desire

Now you've learned all about your product and you're sure it's the one for you, it's time to create passion and desire for what you're selling. It *is* a competitive world out there. Lots of different products and services are flaunting themselves, trying to get the buyer's attention, and you have to make sure you stand out from the crowd. Part of how you'll do this is through enthusiasm for your product. Because you genuinely love what you're selling, you'll be able to naturally stimulate enthusiasm in others.

However, we're going to pour a bit of cold water on that now. Buyers are sold to in all sorts of ways on a daily basis, and they're often too busy to stop and listen to what you have to say about your product. Let's listen to how a buyer feels about the massive amount of sales contact most businesses receive today:

BUYER'S VIEWPOINT: In an average week I receive about three sales calls and two or three pieces of junk mail. I also get my fair share of spam emails. I have no idea how they find me, but I receive about ten sales emails a day. A lot of this contact is relevant to me and offers me products I might have an interest in. But because there's so much of it, it's very hard to remember any one call, email or letter in any detail.

Later on, we'll talk about how to develop 'nutshell' statements that will really get your buyer's attention. But more generally, how do you get your voice heard above the thousands of others in this competitive marketplace? We'd like you to tap into the creative part of yourself and get you thinking about ways to make your product stand out and to achieve an audience with a buyer. It doesn't have to be anything too outlandish – just something that pushes you above the other sellers in the pile.

DAVID: We're actually not aiming to get your buyer to fall head-over-heels in love with what you're offering the first time they hear about it. Your intention should not be to sell when you first talk to buyers. What you're hoping to do is stimulate curiosity. You need to get your buyer thinking that what you're selling might, just might, be something of interest to them. One of the best examples I've got of someone being creative to stimulate curiosity is Julia Ray. She sent her CV to me, but nobody ever read it. It sat in a pile of other unread CVs on my desk. So she sent me a pocket plant. And it came special delivery to the office with a note that said, 'I'll phone you at 11 a.m. tomorrow, love Julia.' Well, what do you think I was doing at 11 a.m. the next day? 'Whoever phones in at 11 for me, I want to speak to her.' And I roared with laughter when she phoned. 'Have I got your full attention now?' she said. 'You need to employ me.' So we did.

Remember: you've already got an advantage. You're sure your product is fantastic and offers unique qualities that make it better than the competition. You genuinely love and are enthusiastic about what you're selling. So relax, you're already doing well. But there's no harm in getting yourself a little extra attention.

DOING IT: How are you going to make your product stand out from the crowd to get an audience with a buyer? There are no rules or word limits here. This is a chance for you to be really inventive and exciting. Remember it's all about curiosity. How can you make buyers curious to know more? What can you send them or say to them to really get their attention? We know you've got some fantastic ideas just waiting to come out!

6

What Are Your Buyers Selling?

Why Learning Your Buyer's Business Is Vital

Do you remember we told you you've already got a great sales personality? And that you sell naturally to family and friends without even trying? What do you think is the big advantage you have when you're persuading a close friend to let you drive their new car, as opposed to selling a photocopier to the MD of a company? We've told you already, so if you were paying attention you should know. We're going to give you a guess...

OK. You'll get a great big gold star if you got this one:

You know your friends and family

You know all sorts of things – their tastes, their fears, their odd little quirks. You know the embarrassing titles in their music collection, the side of the bed they like to sleep on and whatever else it is that makes them unique. This is a major ingredient of great selling. Let's say it out loud:

Know your buyer!

You won't be a great seller unless you learn about your buyers' businesses before you start selling. By this, we mean you should know who is likely to need what you're selling and why. Then find out as much as you can about them before you sell. Yes, you *can* try to sell to anyone and everyone without finding out who they are and what they do, and the law of averages says eventually you'll stumble across people who need your product. But when you do, it's going to be very difficult to have a straight, honest conversation about what your product can do for them if you know nothing about their business.

> LUCY: There's a difference between being a great seller and a seller who just about gets by. Have you ever heard the phrase 'Activity drives revenue'? It's true to an extent, but only if it's the right activity. Great sellers find the right potential customers and target them with the right message. Sometimes salespeople work really hard just so they feel they're doing something, but they're really wasting a lot of time talking to the wrong people. When they miss their target they can then say, 'Well, it's not for lack of doing.'

When businesses are approached by salespeople, they really want a seller who has done their own research in their own time. They don't want to pay someone for the privilege of learning about whatever it is they do. Any seller who already knows about our business at meta-morphose before they make contact with us has a massive advantage. We're more than happy to talk to someone who's well informed about what we might need and knows enough about meta-morphose to have a proper, intelligent discussion about our requirements.

How to Find Your Perfect Partner

How do you work out which businesses need your product or service and track them down? It's a bit like online dating. You need to think about people who have similar interests and might like what you have to offer. There's an element of intuition here. You've probably already got an idea of who might be interested in your product or service. It's just a question of focusing and getting your thoughts out on paper.

> **DOING IT:** Write down the three types of business most likely to need your product or service on a regular basis. What do these businesses do and what sector do they operate in? Don't let us stop you at three. If you can think of more, fantastic!
>
> 1
> 2
> 3

Now you've focused on who your perfect business partners are, how do you find them? You probably know much more than we do about where to find the specific businesses that need *your* product.

> **DOING IT:** Remember those three business types we asked you to think of? We'd like you to find real-life examples of each of these types of business, including addresses and phone numbers.
>
> 1
>
> 2

3

If you need a bit of inspiration, listen to how a member of the meta-morphose team looks for potential buyers.

BETH: There are so many different ways to source new clients. I look at newspapers to get a flavour of what's going on in business, check recruitment adverts for information, search Google, talk to meta-morphose trainees and other business contacts, ask friends, visit exhibitions – really the possibilities are endless and I'm always discovering new methods of finding buyers.

DOING IT: Now you've found three companies, let's discover more about them. You probably won't be able to find out what side of the bed they sleep on, but you can glean a lot of other things. See if you can find out the following about your companies:

Do they have a specific department that deals with your product or service?
Are they expanding at the moment or are they looking to cut costs?
How big are they?
Do they use suppliers from other countries?

It's a courtesy to find out what you can about a business before you make contact, and the answers to these questions will also give you a flavour of what your potential buyer might need. Better still, the more you learn about the company you're selling to, the better results you're likely to achieve. Let's look at an example of how a meta-morphose team member got great results by getting to know his buyer's business.

RICH: I always find out as much as possible about a company before and during the sales process, and the more research I do the better results I tend to get. When I won a £2.7 million sale with a government department, I'd literally spent two years getting to know all about the buyer and what they required before I actually got to the position where I could sell. Not only did I secure the sale, they thanked me for finding out so much about them and helping them through the sales process.

It's good to be prepared, but remember you also need instinct and intuition when you're selling. You can learn a lot about companies and prepare in all sorts of ways, but your natural feelings are also an excellent guide when you're talking to buyers. Don't forget to listen to those feelings! You can never know everything about a company, and even the most experienced salespeople don't have a magic method of finding out the full story about a client before they meet them.

DAVID: Lucy, do you remember the time we gave a sales presentation to that law firm in London? At the time, we considered ourselves experienced salespeople who knew a few things about researching buyers in advance. We researched this law firm as much as we could, and we assumed the presentation would run smoothly as usual. This was around the time PowerPoint presentations were really taking off, and everyone was using them. I've never really been one for visual aids - I prefer to paint pictures with words – but on this occasion a visual was called for, so I grabbed a flip chart and started drawing a few sketches in marker pen to illustrate my point. We didn't feel the presentation went too well, and the feedback we had afterwards was that this law firm thought it was appalling. Why? Because we didn't have a PowerPoint presentation! You can research the ins and outs of any company in advance, but there are some things you just can't know. Of course, immediately after that feedback I enrolled on a PowerPoint course and became an expert. I can do fantastically elaborate computer presentations now, with bits whizzing across the screen and everything. Have my PowerPoint abilities ever won me a sale? I don't think so, and these days PowerPoint isn't even the big thing any more.

There's no point worrying out things you can't know, but it is important to find out all you can before you start selling.

Part II

Getting Into It –
The Sales Process in Action

It's All About REPEC – Sell in Five Easy Steps

This is where things really start to hot up, because now you've done the preparation we're going to teach you how to sell. In fact, we're going to teach you the best way to sell. By learning REPEC, the meta-morphose five-step selling framework, you'll be teaching yourself the guidelines used by every top seller – whether they realise they use them or not. With REPEC, we've pretty much distilled years of sales experience, consultation and experimentation into one handy set of guidelines. Believe us, we wish this is something we had when we were sales virgins. It would have saved us a lot of time, trouble and indecent exposure.

Let's remind you what REPEC stands for by taking a look at the five stages:

Rapport: Building a relationship with your buyer and establishing trust
Explore: Asking the right questions to find out all about your buyer
Position: Showing the buyer how your product meets their needs
Expand: Checking you've matched the buyer's needs correctly
Commit: Closing the sale

We're here to tell you this is the path everyone follows when they complete a sale successfully, and it's the most effective set of guidelines any sales virgin can have. Listen to what one of our sales trainees has to say about it.

GARETH: I've been extremely lucky to attend meta-morphose sales training and learn the REPEC sales stages. They're general to all of industry and gave me an excellent foundation on which to start my sales career. After learning REPEC I instantly began to see results. Conversations were more in depth and I found myself doing a great deal more listening rather than just talking. By understanding each stage of the sales process and learning to empathise with buyers, I sell more effectively and target key benefits to individual needs.

When sales goes wrong for whatever reason, even in the case of experienced salespeople, we can guarantee one thing: the person hasn't gone through all the stages of REPEC. And we can also guarantee that when sales goes fantastically well, when sellers are massively exceeding their targets, winning awards and raking in sizeable amounts of commission, they're following each stage of the REPEC framework.

Not only does REPEC offer a set of guidelines to follow and handy signposts to stop you getting lost during a sale, it also offers a logical, scientific system that allows you to work out how to get better and better. OK, it's not *that* scientific, but REPEC is a bit like a working prototype. If you know something works and keep it consistently the same, you can experiment with making it suit you and work your way – and, of course, improve and earn even more success.

As with any learning and self-improvement, you're likely to make mistakes along the way, so it's great to have a path to follow that you know works. As long as you're following the REPEC stages, it'll be much easier to spot what's going wrong and what's working really well. When you're a sales superstar, making twice as much commission as everyone else on the team, you want to know exactly how you're making everything work so you can keep on doing it.

But don't let us baffle you with science (as if we would). REPEC really is very simple, just like everything else about selling. In fact, REPEC is a slightly more complicated version of the very basic fundamentals of selling:

Find out what someone wants
Show them how to get it
...and they'll buy.

It's important to remember that at the heart of REPEC lies this very simple formula, because salespeople often forget the basics and this is where sales goes wrong. If there's something we drum into our trainees over and over again, it's 'remember the basics'. And when they're experienced salespeople we say, 'You haven't forgotten the basics, have you?' Stick to the basics and you can't go too far wrong. As soon as you overcomplicate selling, you'll wander off the path and stop doing as well as you should.

Before we launch into the first stage of REPEC and get you learning how to establish great rapport with buyers, we'd just like to make it really clear we're not giving you concrete rules to learn in a rigid way. REPEC, just like everything else in this book, is a set of guidelines for you to make your own.

LUCY: REPEC isn't a set of rules or a script. We don't believe selling should ever be so calculated or impersonal. It's more like a framework to be guided by. As I often *say to my trainees, it's something to hang your hat on - but we're not going to tell you which hat to wear.*

However, REPEC should be used completely, and by this we mean you have to follow all the stages through from beginning to end. You can't pick off the bits you want and mix them up.

How to Learn REPEC

At meta-morphose, we start off by loading REPEC onto our trainees so they know exactly what it's all about. But it's really a bit too much to take in at first, so the next thing we do is go over and over everything until it's second nature. And that's what we encourage you to do with Part II of this book: go over and over it until you don't even have to think about what you're doing.

LUCY: The meta-morphose course loads REPEC onto trainees on the first day. Then we spend the rest of the week going through it stage by stage, carrying out role playing and exercises. Friday is when we pull everything together and take trainees through the complete sales presentation.

Just like our courses, this book is really hands on and there's a lot of work to do. Our intention is to get you *doing*, and although we can't replicate for you exactly what we put our graduates through at meta-morphose (and we might even tell you what that is by the end of the book), we will get you into the action as much as possible. So let's get straight to it, starting with the first 'R' of REPEC: 'rapport'.

7

Rapport – Building a Relationship

When we talk about 'rapport', we basically mean 'getting on' with someone – ideally the person you're selling to. Truly great sellers are brilliant at building rapport with customers. In fact, when you see a good seller at work, their customers always walk away feeling fantastic – even if they didn't make a purchase. The buyer may not remember the seller's name, what they looked like or how they carried themselves; they just know they had a good experience. On the other hand, some sellers can make a perfectly good job of presenting their product, but have little impact on the buyer. How do some sellers interest buyers and make them feel great? Not only are we going to tell you, we're going to show you how to do it yourself.

When we ask our trainee groups to sell us on rapport and tell us why it's the most important part of REPEC (but remember, no part of REPEC is more important than another!), they usually tell us relating to buyers as human beings is vital, before you can even think about selling. And they're right. Rapport is the essential first step to selling and your whole sale will be on the wrong footing without it.

LUCY: If you're selling a truly unique product, you might be able to do it without building rapport. But there aren't many unique products on the market these days. It's pretty unusual to have no competitors and that's great – because it means there's room for you and I to do the fantastic job of building rapport. It's essential (and very enjoyable) to build a relationship with your buyer before you start probing them about their business needs and presenting your product. And rapport with customers is part of what makes our products attractive. So learn how to do it and you'll boost the appeal of whatever you're selling without any price cuts, special offers or product enhancements.

We tell our trainees all the time they must build a relationship with somebody before they get into the selling process; if you want to call it a process (and we prefer not to). It should be relationship first, sale second. Always. Treating people as individuals is a vital part of ethical selling, and of course, as we've already explained, ethical selling is effective selling.

As a salesperson, there are two ways to build rapport with a new buyer:

1. Give your buyer a really good reason to talk to you
2. Earn your buyer's trust

Let's take a look at the first one right now.

How to Get Noticed

The first time you talk to a new buyer, it's highly likely you'll be doing so on the telephone. Most salespeople introduce themselves to or 'prospect' for future clients by simply picking up the telephone and calling companies. At metamorphose, our sales team dedicates a lot of time to prospecting. You learned how to find your perfect buyer partners in Chapter 6. Now you're going to learn how grab their attention within the first few seconds of your call.

Buyers Are Busy People

When you're contacting new prospects by telephone, it's vital to remember your buyers are busy people with lives of their own. They weren't staring at the phone waiting for your call, and they don't feel they owe you a moment of their time. If you were dating, you could compare your buyer to a gorgeous celebrity with a knock-out body and several dates lined up, whereas you're just an average person hoping for a moment of their time. Don't assume you automatically deserve a buyer's attention – you should earn it by quickly and interestingly explaining exactly why they might want to talk to you.

BUYER'S VIEWPOINT: Apart from half an hour with a cup of coffee first thing in the morning, my day is absolutely packed. I'm on the go until at least 6.30 p.m. every evening, sometimes later. I don't mind receiving sales calls if they're short and to the point, but I really resent having my time taken up by salespeople who waffle on about what they have to offer for five minutes without stopping for breath. If someone's got something succinct, relevant and interesting to say, then fine. They might actually save me time in the long run.

Give a Really Great Reason for Your Call

So how do we raise the interest level from 'You're not even in my world' to 'You might, just might have something that will benefit me'? You have to give a great reason for your call within 30 seconds of making contact with a buyer.

LUCY: The buyer always comes first. When you're on the telephone and making an outbound cold call, whatever *the buyer is doing is more important than your call. And however you contact a buyer, their head will be full of what's going on with their day. So you have to give them a really strong reason to talk to you. That governs everything. If you haven't got a really good reason to interrupt someone's day, what are you doing talking to them in the first place?*

In order to grab someone's attention quickly, you need to plan what you're going to say. We don't mean write a script exactly, but you should have a clear idea of how to say several things at once and really make an impact in a very short sentence. Within 30 seconds you need to:

- Offer a product benefit
- Get your buyer interested in finding out more

Really, we're talking about a good old-fashioned chat-up line. To raise someone's interest within 30 seconds of talking to them, you should really make every word count. Save your buyer time and plan what's going to interest them before you make contact. OK, so maybe chat-up lines went out in the 1980s, but with sales there's still a place for a good line to reel someone in – as long as you don't stick to it slavishly. Don't get too tied to a particular approach or forget you're talking to a human being and it'll work wonders.

Let's look at examples of chat-up lines used by the metamorphose team when they talk to buyers for the first time. Remember, these aren't written in stone. They're just to give you a feeling of what our team tends to say when they call buyers.

DAN: I'd like to talk to you about how we could increase the efficiency of your sales team. We work with lots of clients in all sorts of different sectors. Can I ask how you usually develop your sales team?

LISA: We identify talented, graduate individuals looking for a career in B2B sales, then give them expert training and turn them into sales superstars. Could this be of interest to you?

ANTONI: We provide B2B sales roles for graduates, giving them 12 months of expert training in order to make them really successful salespeople. What's your current process for attracting salespeople to your organisation?

And a more general line from David:

DAVID: I don't know if this is good for you or not, but we deal with companies like yours. We've managed to make companies like yours pots of money. Could I ask you about yourself?

What do these chat-up lines have in common?

- First and foremost, they're honest. In each case, the salesperson is honest about the purpose of their call.
- They're short. Your chat-up line should be able to entice and excite within seconds. What most people do on a cold call is launch into a 'mini sale'. But it's much better to keep it short, sweet and to the point.
- They don't assume that whoever is on the other end of the phone will definitely be interested. You wouldn't strut up to a total stranger and say 'Get your coat baby,

you've pulled' (or at least we hope you wouldn't), so please don't do the sales equivalent by saying 'This product is perfect for you' before you've even found out someone's name.

- They give a good reason for the call. This is key to rapport. Your chat-up line has to contain a great reason, otherwise you've got no business talking to a buyer in the first place.
- They all naturally lead onto the next stage of REPEC, which is the questioning phase: 'explore'.

What we're referring to as chat-up lines here, we usually call 'nutshell statements' at meta-morphose. But they're the same thing. A short, snappy line that grabs the attention and gets the buyer thinking you could have something really useful to them.

> DAVID: When we talk about 'nutshell statements', sometimes people suggest they're a bit old hat. Well, yes, possibly they are. But for virgins, how else do you start? They've got to be stimulating, tasty and sexy, otherwise they're nothing but a yawn.

Your chat-up line should be interesting and original. It's worth bearing in mind that when you call a potential buyer, you're unlikely to get through to the key person you need to speak to straight away. In the business world there are so many barriers to get through: voicemail, email, PAs... So your chat-up line needs to be extra specially fantastic in order to stimulate interest.

DOING IT: Grab a copy of your local paper and take a look at the lonely hearts ads. Which are the ads that really get your attention and why? Chances are, the ads that make you look twice are original and to the point. Let's take an example:

ATTRACTIVE, tall man, looking for woman with good sense of humour for romance, socialising and cosy nights in.

It's alright, but it doesn't exactly set the world on fire. How about this one:

FREE to a good home. Fab forty something with own litter tray would love to meet fellow cat lover.

It certainly gets the attention, even if this fab forty something isn't for you.

Make a note of two ads that really make you take notice and try to decide what it is that's so interesting about them. There are no rules here – note whatever ads you feel work well. Then have a think about why they're effective and make some notes if you need to.

Remember also to be honest, sincere and courteous. If someone doesn't have time to talk to you, then respect that. You
can always make a date to speak to them another time.

DOING IT: Now it's time to design your own chat-up line. In
40 words or fewer, write a succinct opening line for a telephone cold call that explains your product benefit, stimu-
lates interest and preferably creates a desire.

You probably won't hit upon your perfect chat-up line
straight away, so try out a number of different variations,
and read them out loud to make sure they trip off the
tongue easily.

Trust Me – I'm a Salesperson!

After you've got someone's attention, the next part of rapport
is all about developing trust. People have to trust the person
they're buying from, particularly in the business world where
purchases often run into thousands of pounds. This stage of
rapport is more usually achieved face to face, after you've
won a sales appointment and have a little more time to talk
to your buyer. However, you should be thinking about build-

ing trust no matter how you approach a client or whatever stage of the sale you're at.

Unless a buyer trusts you, the sale is going nowhere. It's a cliché, but people buy from people. If they don't trust the person in front of them, it's highly unlikely they're going to buy. Now you may be thinking, 'Is it possible to build trust with a perfect stranger in the short space of a phone call or sales appointment?' The answer is yes, yes, yes!

Trust or Like?

What's more important: trust or like? Do you have to *like* the person you're buying from? What do you think?

When we ask our trainees whether you have to like the person you're buying from, usually the majority of them think that you do. After all, isn't rapport about getting along with people? Well, it is and it isn't. It's great if people like you when you're helping them to buy, but we actually think trust is much more important.

> LUCY: When we first meet people, we get an instantaneous sense of whether we trust them or not. This is much more important than likeability. Believe it or not, I don't think you have to be liked by a buyer in order to sell, but they must trust and respect you, which is what the second part of building rapport is all about. Of course, there's no reason why they shouldn't like you too - it certainly doesn't hurt!

You don't have to be everyone's best friend in order to sell to them. In fact, most people find it quite irritating when salespeople try to be their friend because, after all, friendships aren't made in minutes. Many salespeople are friends with buyers they've developed relationships with over the years, but when you're meeting a buyer for the first time remember: trust can be established quickly, but friendship shouldn't be rushed.

LUCY: A salesman came to look at my computer system recently, but unfortunately I was really late for a meeting when he called round. I explained this to him and apologised as I tried to rush out the door, but just as I was about to make an exit he said, 'So, how are you today?'

'Fine!' I said, 'but I really have to...'

'It's a lovely day, isn't it?' he continued. 'Have you got any kids?'

'Yes!' I said, feeling an increasing sense of urgency.

'Aw, bless. What are their names?'

I told him, though gritted teeth, and eventually managed to make my excuses and leave. I could see this man thinking 'God, what a terrible mother!' and needless to say we didn't end the meeting best of friends. But then I'd never asked for anything more than a business relationship...

First Impressions

So how do great salespeople establish trust in a buying situation? First and foremost, they think about first impressions. Here's another cliché (sorry): you never get a second chance to make a first impression. True? Not always. But this saying is probably more true for salespeople, who often only have minutes to make any impression at all. We don't always get another go at getting it right. Salespeople need to establish rapport quickly, and a lot of building trust actually happens within the first few seconds of meeting a new buyer.

When we meet someone for the first time face to face, studies show we weigh up three things within a few split seconds. For a buyer, these three things affect how they feel about you as a salesperson, and whether they're open to building trust and rapport with you or not. These are:

- What you say
- How you look
- How you sound

Of these three things, which do you think is most important to making a good first impression? Let's take a look:

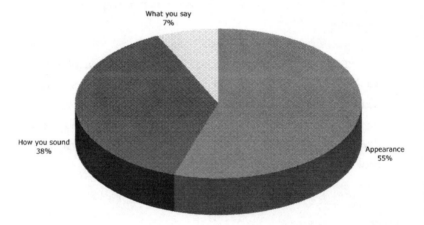

So studies suggest people predominantly judge others by their appearance when it comes to first impressions. In fact, it's believed this judgement is made within the first 30 seconds of meeting someone, and of course for a salesperson it's pretty vital this judgement is favourable. People are very amenable to changing their mind in the long term, but salespeople don't always have time to change people's minds.

Sales appointments are usually 20 minutes or half an hour long, if we're lucky.

DAVID: It's impossible to overestimate how important a first impression is – just be sure you get it as near right as you can and leave no room for mistakes. You can never be overdressed, just incorrectly dressed.

Appearance isn't just about how we're dressed. It's about body language too. At meta-morphose, we break it down into four elements:

- Clothes and presentation
- Eye contact
- Handshake
- Smile

A buyer has to recognise quickly that you're a confident professional with something important to discuss. It's therefore very important you offer lots of eye contact, a firm, warm handshake, and smile and present yourself professionally. Imagine seeing someone across a crowded room. They look great, but when you approach them they look at the floor, hunch their shoulders and don't offer to shake your hand. Sexy? Not in the slightest.

Good body language and tone of voice really come down to confidence. If you feel confident, you stand up a little straighter, make more eye contact, sound calmer and look happier. Because you've got something great to offer, you should already feel confident about talking to buyers face to face. However, because you're still a virgin you may feel a little nervous at first. Don't worry! You'll become confident very quickly when your commissions start to roll in. Also, you'll probably have a lot of success over the telephone before you start having face-to-face meetings with clients, so you'll have plenty of opportunity to practise your tone of voice without worrying about visual elements. If you still feel you need a boost, there's a handy section in Part III which will help push your confidence sky high. In the meantime, here are some hints about looking great and sounding sexy.

You Look Great!
The best way to dress is like a business professional, and ideally how you present yourself should match your buyer and their industry. If in doubt, it's best to opt for more formal attire.

> DOING IT: Think about how people present themselves in the industry you're selling to. Use five words to describe the people in your industry. We'll give you some examples: fun, down-to-earth, hardworking, serious, professional, intelligent, specialist... We're sure you can think of some even better ones:
>
> 1
> 2
> 3
> 4
> 5
>
> Now, have a think about an outfit that sums up these words. We'd love to give you some pictures, but our ideas about how to dress you might not fit your own. Remember to use your instincts and inner judgement about what is most appropriate to wear for the people you're meeting.

Sounding Sexy

If 38% of a first judgement made about you is based on how you sound rather than what you say, how do great sales-people make sure they sound sexy within the first few moments of speaking to someone? This is particularly important for sales virgins, since it's more than likely a lot of first contact with buyers will be over the telephone. And you'll be pleased to know sounding sexy is very simple. In fact, you'll automatically sound sexy if you:

- Know your buyer
- Know your product
- Get your chat-up line ready to go
- Are honest and sincere

If you've worked out how to interest a buyer and can speak openly, honestly and knowledgeably about your product and industry, your voice will already sound assured and intelligent. Knowing your product inside out means you can communicate intelligently with your buyer, without stumbling over your words or giving assurances you'll find something out later. As an extra bonus, because you've got a great product you know all about, you'll also be *saying* something worthwhile – if anyone's paying attention!

How to Be More Loveable

Now let's look at the second part of building trust: listening to your buyer and bending to see things from their point of view. Good communicators flex to become a little bit more like whoever they're talking to, and great salespeople are great communicators: it's as simple as that. Next time you see a good communicator in action, in a sales situation or just an everyday conversation, notice how they focus on the other person and try to get on their wavelength. It's really a question of putting the other person first and letting them take charge of the conversation.

DAVID: I've always been fascinated by how really great salespeople interact with customers. As a consultant, I was lucky enough to observe hundreds of exceptional salespeople and really get to grips with how they build rapport with buyers. Great salespeople don't try to be everyone's best friend. They're simply interested in the people they're selling to, and have the ability to put their own ego on the shelf while they're learning about their buyer. We're all pleased when someone shows an interest in us. Often, the most unlikely people at a party can be surrounded by people chatting them up, simply because they listen and don't talk about themselves. They don't expect anything from anyone and readily accept other people around them.

In order to be a good communicator, you must have a good empathy/ego balance. By this we mean your ego is well-balanced and in control, and you don't expect everyone else to think you're wonderful. Instead, you think about things from other people's points of view and let go of your own need to feel important.

DAVID: Empathy means understanding someone, and really sharing their concerns and feelings in order to see things from their point of view. When you empathise, you're accepting people and allowing them to be themselves.

As a salesperson, it's your job to listen and empathise. You don't have to pretend you agree with everything your buyer is saying, but you *should* flex slightly and get into their opinions and ways of doing things. You shouldn't contradict the person you're selling to, and you should express understanding of their currency and values. After all, if you want to influence someone you have to go by their rules, measures and ideals. This is what makes the difference between OK sellers and great sellers.

LUCY: When we meet people for the first time, we ask ourselves two questions:
   Do I trust you?
   Are you my sort of person?
And what we really want in a salesperson is... well, some-one who's a bit like us. Good salespeople instinctively judge who's in front of them, or on the end of the tele-phone, and flex their behaviour just enough to get on the buyer's wavelength and build trust.

When salespeople fail to develop rapport and empathy with their customer, it's almost always down to the same things: not empathising and not listening. Salespeople often have plenty to talk about and want to get all enthusiastic about their product before they've found out anything about a customer. Now, enthusiasm is really great and we don't want you to lose any of it, but let us tell you the best way to build rapport:

Listen much more than you talk.

In fact, we've got a formula for just how much you should listen *throughout* the whole sale:

Listen 70% of the time, and talk 30%.

We all have opinions and we all like to tell people how much we know (well, most of us, anyway), but as a salesperson your job is mainly to *listen* and *empathise*. You'll learn even more about the importance of listening when we get to the next stage of REPEC and talk about exploring your customer's needs.

Instinct, not Stereotype

Great salespeople listen to their instincts when they're working out how to communicate with buyers. They don't think in stereotypes. We probably all make assumptions about others, and equally we all hate assumptions being made about us – even if they're correct. As a salesperson, the rule is simple: don't judge others before you've spoken to them.

LUCY: A lot of car salespeople assume women care about the colour of the car they're buying, and you've barely said hello before they're asking you your favourite colour. This really irritates me and I always find it very tempting to pretend I don't care about colour at all. I actually think a lot of women do mind about the colour of their car, but they pretend not. Who likes assumptions being made about them? It's vital to let the customer tell you what's important to them, because any preconceived ideas you have – right or wrong – are unlikely to be welcome.

Now you know the basics of building great rapport with buyers. Well done! You should be really pleased with your progress. It's time to get really nosy and find out all about your buyer. Let's move on to the next stage of REPEC: 'explore'.

8

Exploration – Asking Buyers about Themselves

Stage two of REPEC is all about exploring what the buyer wants by asking the right questions and listening carefully to the answers. If you're even a little bit nosy, you're going to love this bit because it means finding out all about someone else's business. Actually, part of exploring your customer should take place before the sale, when you research their business, products and industry. But during the sale itself is your golden opportunity to find out *exactly* what makes your buyer tick.

If you're going to do a great job of positioning your product during stage three of REPEC (and we know you will), you need to do fantastically well at exploring your buyer beforehand. You need to make sure what you're presenting to them is totally relevant to their needs, and to do this you need to ask the right questions and listen carefully to the answers. Basically, you've got to really get into bed with your buyer.

Why It's Great to Be Nosy
When you're exploring and using all the right questions, you're essentially doing two things:

1. Finding out which buying stage your customer is at.
2. Exploring your buyer in relation to each buying stage.

Do you remember the five buying stages? We covered them in Chapter 4 and they are:

1. Present Reality – The Comfort Zone
2. Issues – Do We Have a Problem Here?
3. Future Map – The Dream Relationship
4. Evaluation – Weighing Up the Pros and Cons
5. Decision – Shall We Make a Commitment?

For someone to buy something, they need to move from one of these stages onto another, and your job as a salesperson is to help them through this process. During the 'explore' phase of REPEC, your questions will determine exactly where your buyer is on the buying map and what they need from your product or service.

It's really important to get to know the buying stages well and to remember your job is to walk alongside buyers as they move through – not to lead. Let's look at each stage in turn, so you see how the right questions will really help you get to grips with your buyer's reality.

Present Reality – the Comfort Zone

If you're coming to a customer cold, the first questions you should ask are about their present reality. Here are some good examples:

- Tell me about your company...
- What are you doing currently?
- Why are you doing things this way?
- How did you get here?

If a buyer is actually in the present reality stage, they'll often tell you they have an existing supplier. You're particularly likely to hear this if you're making a cold call: 'We've already got a supplier, and we're very happy, thank you very much.'

The thing is, people might *say* they're happy with their existing supplier. But often when you get talking to them you'll find out that actually they've had all sorts of problems with their supplier for years, and you can offer them something much better.

> LUCY: If someone tells me they have an existing supplier, I usually say something like: 'Great! If you're totally happy, then there's nothing we can offer you. But can I ask you how well that's working for you at the moment?'

As a salesperson, your role is to show customers a need they possibly weren't aware of and then demonstrate how you can meet that need. Of course, if their existing supplier totally meets their needs and their budget, then wish them all the best and walk away from the sale – at least for now. But you'd be surprised how many people in the 'comfort zone' will change their supplier if approached in the right way.

Issues – Have We Got a Problem Here?

Once you've established a buyer's present reality, you should be looking for the gaps or problems with what they're doing at the moment. You also need to work out how big these problems are and how willing the buyer is to change things. Some good questions to establish this are:

- What would cause you to change?
- How big an issue is this for you?
- What is the impact of the current situation?

DAVID: Buyers will usually tell you if they have an issue with how something is currently working, but sometimes they might do so very subtly. I've had buyers tell me things like: 'If I don't get this done by this date, there'll be trouble.' Which might mean: 'I'm not 100% confident our current supplier will deliver on time.'

Future Map

Once you've talked about issues with a buyer, you need to ask them about the solution. A major mistake salespeople make is to hear a problem, then impress upon the buyer their own solution – without actually bothering to ask for the buyer's opinion. We've said it before and we'll say it again: buyers aren't stupid. If they've got issues with the way things are working, they'll often have an ideal solution mapped out. From a seller's point of view this is brilliant, because you can ask buyers exactly what the perfect solution is to their problem. So some good questions to ask are:

- What does an ideal solution look like to you?
- What do you want to do instead?

DAVID: It's a classic mistake for sellers not to ask what a buyer wants, then launch straight into the comfort zone of presenting their product. People often know exactly what they want, what they really, really want – and they'll tell you if you ask. Sometimes salespeople are so caught up with selling with a capital S, they forget to put their ego on the shelf and just ask a buyer for the solution.

Evaluation: Weighing up Pros and Cons

Now you need to talk about the other options a buyer may have available to them, such as other suppliers or using in-house resources. There *is* competition out there, whether you like it or not, and at some point your buyer is going to be looking at solutions that don't involve you. Salespeople are often uncomfortable finding out about the competition and don't relish the prospect of talking through the other options a buyer may be considering. But thinking about different options is an essential part of what people do when they buy. So it's an essential consideration for sellers too.

LUCY: Talking about the different options buyers consider is a vital part of selling. Often salespeople don't ask about alternatives because they're scared a buyer might work out they don't need them. But as a seller you should know the options a buyer is considering, because you'll lose sales if you don't know. If you don't discuss alternatives with a buyer, you can guarantee as soon as your back is turned they'll be discussing them anyway. And you need to know the whole picture if you're going to sell your product effectively. I'd rather find out from a buyer just what they're weighing up than lose a sale.

So you should be asking:

- What alternatives are you considering?
- What's important to you from a supplier?
- What do we have to do to stand out?

Decision – Shall We Make a Commitment?

Finally, you need to ask buyers about how they're going to make the final buying decision. As a seller, you need to find out exactly who the chief decision maker is and the budgets and timescales involved. If there are influential decision makers you didn't find out about, or budget issues you weren't aware of, you'll be in no position to sell effectively and you could lose the sale.

> LUCY: I've been selling for 23 years, and when I started out it was much easier to get through to the chief decision maker. Now there are whole purchasing departments involved in buying, and they all have different decision makers, influencers and budgets to consider. So it's vital you ask the right questions to find out all the factors involved, and don't assume whoever you're talking to has the final say.

The kinds of questions you should now be asking are:

- How will a decision be made?
- Who will be involved?
- What budgets and timescales are involved with this decision?

Mixing Things Up

There are two sorts of questions you can use while you're selling: open questions and closed questions. Closed questions always have a 'yes' or 'no' answer, and they're very useful for getting short, sharp facts. For example:

- Would you like to go to dinner with me?

- Do you like Japanese food?
- Shall we meet outside the pub?

Some examples of closed questions that will help you learn more about your customer are:

- Do you have a supplier at the moment?
- Are you happy with your current supplier?
- Do you have to make a decision within a certain timescale?

Open questions invite much more information and tend to begin with how, where, why, when, what and who. Here are some examples:

- Tell me about yourself...
- What do you really love?
- What's important to you?

And here are some open questions that should help you find out more about your customer:

- How do you choose your suppliers?
- Who makes the decisions about suppliers?
- What do you want from a new supplier?

By asking a mixture of open and closed questions, you'll keep your questioning fresh and your buyer energised. It's much more interesting to ask a mixture of questions requiring both long and short answers than a steady stream of either open or closed questions.

DAVID: In selling, you should essentially be saying to a buyer: 'Tell me all about yourself, and your business in relation to what I've got to sell.' But that's a bit basic. There are better ways to chat up your buyer, and that's where a really interesting mix of questions comes in.

If you need convincing that questions are vital for effective selling, try this for size – we promise that every sale you lose will be for one of these five reasons:

1. You haven't understood where the buyer is in the buying stages.
2. You haven't found out a big enough issue for the buyer to want to change what they're doing.
3. The buyer had a great solution in their head and you didn't ask for it.
4. There were hidden decision makers and you didn't find out about them.
5. The problem never existed in the first place.

So of the five reasons why sales are lost, four are largely down to sellers not asking the right questions (and one is fairly unavoidable). If you explore a buyer with the right questions, you'll rule out four of the five major reasons why sellers lose sales. Those are some good odds.

DOING IT: Although we've suggested some good ideas for questions, you should really think up your own way of saying things so you'll sell in a unique, genuine way. It's a good idea to have your own questioning bank, a stock of your personal questions that match each of the buyer stages. Here's one for you to fill in:

1. Present Reality – the Comfort Zone

2. Issues – Do We Have a Problem Here?

3. Future Map – the Dream Relationship

4. Evaluation – Weighing up the Pros and Cons

5. Decision – Shall We Make a Commitment?

How to Stop, Look and *Listen*!

OK, so you've asked the right questions. Now you've simply got to listen to the answers. We've already explained you build great rapport with a buyer by listening. But more fundamentally, your job as a salesperson is to understand buyers by being a great listener. Read what one of our meta-morphose graduates has to say about listening.

> FEARNE: When I applied for the National Sales Awards, they asked me about the most important skills I had as a salesperson. And I told them, 'Being a good listener.' Understanding the client's needs and ensuring these needs are met is what selling is all about. meta-morphose taught me how to listen, and this is a totally invaluable part of sales training.

There's an old adage about salespeople having the gift of the gab, and sometimes we'll get the odd 'potential salesperson' attending an interview with us who thinks selling is all about the patter. If we meet anyone who's truly interested in a sales career and thinks fast talking is what it's all about, we have to re-educate them – quickly! The best sellers are much more likely to be quiet and inquisitive.

Just like being on a date, you should be getting to know your buyer and showing interest in them. It's the most flattering thing in the world to have someone pay close attention to everything you're saying, and as a salesperson you should be the most charming and considerate date around. You should think of the 'explore' stage as saying to someone: 'Tell me all about yourself.' And believe us, there's nothing sexier.

DAVID: Try this. Next time you're at a party and someone asks you what you do, just say: 'It's great. Can't remember what it is, but it's great. Now what do you do?' You should be doing the same thing when you sell. It's all about the buyer and how you can help them, and the only time you should be talking is to tell a buyer exactly how you can meet the needs they've just outlined.

Listening accurately is possibly the most important skill in the whole sales process. Even if everything went horribly wrong in a sale, if you've listened accurately you can go over your notes, work out what your buyer wants and go back and try again.

DAVID: If you're a good listener, you'll sometimes find during a sale that something amazing happens: buyers start to sell to themselves. I've been in several sales situations where all I've done is shut up and let the buyer talk about themselves, and by the time they've finished they've talked themselves into the sale. While I'm listening to them, they change from saying 'We want X and Y, if you can provide it' to 'We want you to do X and Y for us' and they start giving out lots of positive buying signals. A less experienced person might observe this and say, 'Well, they're just a natural salesperson.' But it's just about being a good listener.

The best bit about selling is, unlike a date, you can make notes about what your buyer is saying. So you can literally write out exactly what they're asking for, and have a really valuable resource when it comes to positioning your product. Always remember to keep a notepad handy and make as many notes as possible.

However, a quick word of warning. Listening may sound easy, but when you're flung into a sales situation for the first time, and sometimes even the five hundredth time, things might not go as planned, nerves take hold and you start talking instead of listening. It's easily done: you're seeing a really big-league potential buyer and you're feeling nervous, so what makes you feel comfortable? Talking about what you know. When salespeople feel under pressure, listening can be the first thing that goes out the window, even though it's one of the most important parts of selling. So always, always remember, no matter what else is happening (unless you've noticed the corner of their office is on fire), listen carefully to your buyer.

DAVID: We train much harder at meta-morphose than in the actual sales game itself, so our trainees are ready for any sales situation. Often, when our trainees are a bit nervous, they start talking more and listening less. In fact, as a sales consultant this is the key problem I've seen with experienced salespeople: when they get nervous they won't shut up! It's a common reaction to being under pressure, so just watch out for it when you're selling for real.

DOING IT: Are you a good listener? Phone up a good friend and say to them: 'Tell me all about what's happening with you.' Your goal is to be able to fill in an events diary about everything they've done in the previous week, and what they intend to do next week. If you can't work this out from what they say initially, you'll have to ask more questions. Keep them short and simple: 'What are you up to next week?' and so on. And just listen. You can't make notes when you're talking to them, so you'll have to really

concentrate on their answers. You should aim to listen 70% and talk 30% of the time. It's not difficult, but you may be surprised how much you have to stop yourself talking.
When the call is over, write up a two-week events diary for your friend and see how well you remembered what they said.

If we had to summarise the explore phase, we'd say: 'Ask the right questions, then shut up and listen!' And if you have any problems remembering to keep quiet, here's a friendly reminder:

9

Positioning – Showing Off Your Best Bits

When you've asked all your questions, you should have a good idea what really turns your buyer on. This is the part where you go over in your head everything you've learned so far, remembering to use your intuition as well as the concrete facts your buyer has told you. You should be saying to yourself: 'OK, what exactly does this buyer want from my product, and what can I fulfil?' You also might have some background intuition going on about your buyer, along the lines of: 'What have I found out about this person? Do they want to make more money? Do they want to impress their boss? What are their values?' And you'll be using everything you've learned, both from your questions and your rapport with the buyer, to decide exactly what your customer wants from you and when they need it by. Ready to learn the art of positioning? Let's get started.

Forward Positioning

When you position your product, you're essentially matching the features of what you have to offer with what you've learned about your buyers' needs. And you're making sure your buyers see exactly what your product can do for them – which means you have to work this out on their behalf.

The 'positioning' stage of REPEC is often the favourite part of the sale for sellers because they get to talk about themselves. Plenty of sellers leap straight into positioning a product without really considering all the information they've just learned – and as a result end up boring the pants off a buyer by telling them all sorts of irrelevant things about their product. For many sellers, positioning their product is the 'comfort zone'. It's the bit that doesn't hold any scary surprises – at least in theory. Asking questions, that's the tricky bit, because sellers don't know what the answers are going to be. So all too often, salespeople race through explore and before they've even digested the hugely valuable information they've just learned, they're into positioning.

DAVID: When you position your product, it's vital to use the information you learned during 'explore', otherwise you've jumped straight into talking about yourself and forgotten all about the buyer. This might sound obvious, but believe me it's easy to get good at asking questions and listening, then totally forget to use the information. This is a really common stumbling block for salespeople. They get the rapport going, ask all the right questions, then say, 'Great, now onto me!' They divorce the buyer from all the good work that's been done so far, and say, 'Hurrah, now let ME talk. Sod all your information – I had to do that to seduce you. But I'd far rather talk about me.' Then they launch into brochure speak that has nothing to do with the previous conversation and they're right in the comfort zone – while totally alienating the buyer. But it's got to be all about the buyer all the way. In the positioning stage, imagine your buyer is giving you the old Bette Midler line in the film 'Beaches': 'Let's stop talking about me and start talking about you. So what do you think about me?'

If you've got a fantastic product and know the benefits inside and out, it's tempting to tell a buyer about all of them. But to do so is to sell *to* someone, rather than walk with them along the buying path.

> DAVID: Sellers are often trained to list the features and benefits of their product, without engaging with what the buyer is after. In their heads, it sounds fantastic to be reeling off a long list of benefits, but the truth is unless you've listened to someone else you're not selling – at least not effectively. In real life, you'd never sit in front of someone and list the activities you did on holiday, one after the other, and there's no place for it in sales either. What turns people on is to say, 'I've listened to you and I can do that bit, but I can't do the other bit.' Honestly and relevance all the way...

It's really, really important to make sure every benefit you talk about is *relevant* to what the buyer has said they wanted. Even if your product can brew coffee whilst simultaneously photocopying and sweeping the floor, if these benefits aren't relevant to your buyer, don't talk about them. So keep it short, keep it relevant and don't waste people's time – they'll thank you for it.

> DAVID: As a recruitment solution, we hear all the time about how terrible recruitment agencies are. And the biggest complaint? 'I told them what I wanted, they listened, then they sent me ten candidates who were nowhere near what I asked for.' In fact, that's probably the single biggest reason why people are wary of recruitment companies. They pretend to listen to clients, then send a whole heap of people to interview and hope something sticks. It happens with estate

agents too: there's so much money at stake that they take buyers to any and every property and just hope one fits the bill. Sounds ridiculous, but it happens.

Giving the Client What They Really, Really Want

If you've explored your buyer properly, positioning is easy and lots of fun because you'll be giving your client what they really, really want. Take a look at your sales notes, remember everything your buyer said – and didn't say – and really think about the exact features of your product that meet their needs. If you've learned your product inside and out during Part I, a whole host of product features and benefits should spring to mind. We've told you one of the best ways to learn is by doing, so we're going to get you learning about feature and benefit matching by doing it right now.

DOING IT: Imagine you're with a buyer. Your buyer is a senior manager for a company of about 500 employees. She's conservatively dressed, and tells you she really enjoys working for her company and feels it's a great organisation to have a long-term career with. She says her company believes in investing in the right products, and doesn't mind spending money as long as it gets good results and value. Now she tells you about what the company would like from a new product:

To get better value from their existing budget
To help the company innovate and try new ways of doing things

She's also got a problem: her company spends too much time doing its day-to-day procedures and would like something that helps it speed up business. She adds that she doesn't want anything that will be complicated or time-consuming to start using, and she doesn't want any nasty surprises.

Match the benefits of your product with this buyer's wish list. There's one catch. At first, you can't look back and check the list of product features and benefits you made in Part I:

Right. Now, if you need to you can check your list of product benefits and try again. (If you don't need to, you get a bit pat on the back from us. Well done!)

If you needed to backtrack and check your notes, this should be a lesson to you – learn your product benefits before you sell. If you're selling over the telephone, you'll be able to look at notes of your product benefits, but you won't be able to think half as quickly and there's no substitute for simply knowing everything backwards and forwards.

LUCY: Just a quick reminder: features are what your product does, and benefits are what they will do for a buyer. You should learn both, telling buyers a relevant feature, then use the phrase 'which means that' to turn it into a benefit:

Our products are made with really durable materials, which means that they'll last much longer than anything you're likely to have had before.

Small Really Is Better...

So you know positioning should be relevant and match what your buyer tells you. But you should also really aim to keep the positioning stage as short as possible, and try to say everything succinctly and to the point.

DOING IT: It's time to cut your benefits. Remember the list of features and benefits you made in Part I? We want you to write each of them again – but half as long. Find short, powerful words to describe what you're offering, and use a thesaurus if necessary. Off you go!

A Friend Recommended You...

If you were asked to go on a blind date, chances are you'd be much more inclined to give it a go if a friend recommended your intended suitor. And it's the same in sales: recommendations about your product, or testimonials, can work wonders. Are there any well-known companies or individuals who use your product and would give a recommendation?

> DOING IT: This is a great opportunity for you to do a bit of market research about your product: phone a few existing customers and ask what they think of your product. Then, assuming they've given good feedback about what you're offering, think about how you can communicate this with buyers when you're discussing product benefits. For example, if a buyer says, 'I'd love a fast turnaround', it would be great to tell them, 'We have a large production team (feature), which means that we offer very fast service (benefit). In fact, so-and-so company tells us one of the main reasons it uses our services is our fast turnaround (testimonial).'

Making Your Product Sexier

Throughout the sales process, it's important to remember selling is fun. And positioning your product is particularly enjoyable because you can make it come alive for buyers. At meta-morphose, we sometimes refer to this as 'painting pictures' for buyers, and what we mean is making something really real for someone else, in a context they understand.

> DAVID: When I'm positioning a product, I try to make all the senses come alive. Once I've got an idea of what the buyer is after, I try to paint for them their dream scenario: a perfect picture of what 'good' really looks,

sounds and feels like for them. I'm giving back to the buyer everything I've seen, heard and felt during the explore phase – but in a way that brings the senses alive.

People mainly use a mixture of three senses when they're taking in information: visual, audio and kinaesthetic. These roughly translate to seeing, hearing and feeling. Most sales-people use the visual senses to communicate, by presenting themselves well, using hand gestures and bringing visual aids when they visit buyers. There's nothing wrong with this – a lot of people use their visual senses over and above audio and kinaesthetic. However, you should also remember to think about what your buyer will hear and feel when you're positioning your product. Go ahead and describe just how sturdy your product is to the touch, and the soft, quiet sounds it makes when you turn it on. Really engage all the senses when you're selling. Use bold, exciting words and paint visual pictures with language and hand gestures.

DOING IT: Remember the buyer you met when you were matching product benefits? Imagine the perfect solution for her: a working day where everything ran exactly as she wanted it to. Now picture yourself as your buyer, with every-thing running just the way she'd like it. Using visual, audio and touchy-feely details, describe just what part your prod-uct or service plays in this dream scenario. Make your description as vivid, exciting and stimulating as possible.

How to Check You've Hit the Spot

You're allowed to do more talking during the positioning stage than probably any of the other stages. But even when you're chatting away, you should still pause regularly to give your buyer the chance to speak and, more importantly, *watch your buyer's responses* to what you're saying.

Have you ever given someone a massage for an aching muscle? You might start out miles away from the right spot, so you ask, 'Am I in the right place?' And whoever you're massaging says, 'Left a bit, right a bit... that's the spot!' That's effectively part of what you're doing while you're positioning your product: moving closer and closer to what the buyer wants.

DAVID: While I'm positioning, I'm doing a subliminal check the whole time to make sure I'm on target. I'm still checking my buyer is OK with me, and that I'm not demeaning their trophies or their position in any way. But I'm also watching and listening to the buyer to make sure what I'm building for them is really taking shape in their mind's eye. I'm metaphorically taking my piece of modelling clay and moulding it and remoulding it depending on their reactions, until it dovetails with what I see, feel and hear that they want. And I'm using my instincts to work out if I'm hitting the spot. Often, what you're doing as a salesperson is making a problem go away for your customer. Your product offers some sort of solution, and while you're positioning you'll feel you're dissolving a problem in your buyer's mind. The problem could be anything, from 'I don't make enough money' or 'we don't do things fast enough here' to 'my wife doesn't understand me'. But whatever it is, if it turns them on you need to show it to them.

Now, if you're lucky your buyer might say something like: 'No, we don't quite want something that size. We need something a bit smaller.' Which effectively means 'Down a bit!' and you can reposition what you're offering, or even jump back into explore and ask some more questions. But your buyer won't necessarily say 'Left a bit' if you're off target, so sometimes you just have to use your instincts to try to work out if you're getting near the right spot. This is something we can't teach you, but we will say this: practice makes perfect. The more you're exposed to selling situations, the more you'll learn and be able to work out when you're getting near the target.

DOING IT: Have a think about the problems your product could solve for customers. It might help solve a general problem, such as financial insecurity within a company, or a more personal problem, such as your buyer achieving more recognition at work. Most products or services were invented to solve some kind of problem, so have a think about this in relation to what you sell. Now write down three problems your product solves and exactly how it solves them:

1

2

3

DAVID: Positioning can be a bit like the game Battleships. You're searching around for what your buyer wants and you might sense (or if you're lucky, your buyer will tell you) you've missed the spot quite a few times before you get a hit. But don't worry. Every time a buyer tells you you're not quite offering what they want, you're getting fantastic information.

Learning exactly what doesn't hit the target will eventually give you a picture of exactly what the buyer wants. If you're watching and analysing your buyer while you're positioning, and giving them plenty of opportunity to offer feedback, you'll soon have the perfect idea of what works for them.

Actually, part of what you're doing in the positioning stage is a bit of pre-handling for the next stage of REPEC: 'expand'. If you haven't realised already, expand is the stage where you handle buyer objections. Don't panic! It's much easier than it sounds. But you can deal with a lot of objections before they arise if you position things well.

When you get started on the expand stage in just a moment, you'll really go over everything to make sure you've hit the buyer's target exactly. But when you're positioning, remember to pay close attention to your buyer's responses and be flexible enough to readjust your presentation to make sure you're hitting the spot.

10

Expand – Getting Looked Up and Down

So now we're at stage four, and we're going to spend more time here than at any of the other stages, because 'expand' is often where sales virgins need the most help and advice. It's also the stage that can make the difference between a very average salesperson and a totally brilliant salesperson. You've got a good rapport going with your buyer, you've asked all the right questions and you've presented your product – whilst paying attention to their responses. Now it's time for you to throw off all your clothes and ask your buyer: 'What do you think?'

Up until this stage, you haven't really had to expose yourself at all and put yourself in line for scrutiny, so as a consequence new salespeople (and some old salespeople too) find the expand stage a real challenge. But it needn't be, and with us to help you through it you'll discover it's actually just as easy as every other part of REPEC.

Expand is the REPEC stage where you're asking for permission before you close the sale. Now, if we remember what REPEC originally stood for when it used to be SEPEC, it might become clearer why the expand stage can seem very intimidating. Do you remember what SEPEC stood for?

Stimulation
Exploration
Penetration
Examination
and… **C**onsummation!

So in the expand stage we're asking buyers for permission to move to consummation. We're asking them to succumb to our advances, and expand is where we make sure they're totally ready to do so before we ask them to jump into bed with us.

It's at this stage, while you're checking your buyer is comfortable with everything, that you might bump into buyer objections. When you're new to sales, buyer objections can look rather overwhelming and scary, but they're not. Believe us, once you've practised a few times, and practised the *right way* to communicate with a buyer during this stage, you'll be taking your clothes off in no time.

Just Ask for It

To start off with, in the expand stage you need to check off everything a buyer wants and simply ask them if it sounds about right. You've already done part of this with your positioning, because (we hope) you've been observing your buyer's reactions to what you're offering and subtly changed your presentation to match their needs. But 'expand' is the moment of truth. Have you got it right? Have you hit the spot? You'll never know unless you ask!

So let's go for it and make the verbal check. This is easy. You simply need to run through exactly how your product matches your buyer's needs, and then ask them if you've hit the spot.

DAVID: At the expand stage, you should have a checklist in your head and you're making sure everything is tickety-boo by going, tick, tick, tick – yes, I've met everything you've asked for. You're saying to your buyer: 'Have I seen, heard and felt accurately? Have I got it right? Let me summarise everything: this is your *primary concern, this is most important to you, these are the things you'd like for your budget and these are the people who need to be involved. And we meet these needs in the following way. Is that right?'*

You're asking your buyer: 'Have I got it right? Have I shown you everything you've asked for?' In fact, here are a few good phrases to use during the expand stage to move things forward – hopefully to the last REPEC stage, 'commit'.

- How does this sound to you?
- How does this look?
- What do you think?

And once again, you have to listen very carefully to your buyer's responses. This might seem a bit full on for the new salesperson. After all, by asking 'Have I got it right?' you're vulnerable to rejection and totally exposed. You've taken everything off, stood there in all your glory and said, 'What do you think? Do you like it?' And it's at this point you're likely to encounter buyer objections.

Buyer Objections

If the positioning stage of REPEC is the comfort zone, then the expand stage is the 'mess it all up' zone (and we sometimes use rather stronger language than that to describe what can happen during expand). Why? Because when you've stripped everything off, your buyer can (and often will) tell you exactly why and how you don't fit the bill. They might tell you what works for them, but they're also likely to tell you what doesn't. They'll probably throw in a few misgivings too, about why possibly buying isn't a great idea for them.

These misgivings and mismatches are what people call 'buyer objections', and they're usually the biggest obstacle between exceeding all your targets in sales, winning all the awards and making a big heap of money.

You're going to be a sales superstar, so you're going to learn to deal with buyer objections totally effortlessly. Actually, let's show you exactly how sales virgins usually see these words:

BUYER OBJECTIONS

This is a big, scary subject when you're new to sales, and probably most new salespeople secretly hope they'll never get an objection. But you will. Every salesperson does at one time or another. They sound a little bit like this:

- 'No, sorry, we've already got a good supplier.'
- 'That sounds too expensive.'
- 'I need to think about this – talk to me in a few weeks.'

Listen to the objections a member of our meta-morphose sales team hears on a daily basis:

> DAN: What are some of the objections I hear regularly? Buyers will tell me they have another supplier, or a preferred supplier list. Or that we're too expensive. And you really have to understand what they're saying and go over exactly what they mean. Don't think objections mean you won't make a sale. They're just an opportunity to get to grips with what your buyer wants.

To the inexperienced salesperson, objections sound like 'no sale'. But this isn't what they mean at all, and you're going to learn how to 'hear' objections properly and handle them easily.

LUCY: If we look at how people buy, it's very unusual for a buyer to see a seller presentation and say, 'Great - I love it, how do I buy?' There can't be many salespeople who've made a cold call and immediately had a buyer saying to them, 'Brilliant, I'll take 20'. You will hear objections. So all sellers need to be able to deal with buyer objections if they're going to be terrific at what they do. In fact, I've only ever twice phoned up a company and received no objections whatsoever. Once I phoned a company about team building and they said, 'What an extraordinary thing. We were just discussing this, can you come in this afternoon?' And the other time was when I cold called David to see if he needed sales trainers...

OK: if you position your product so brilliantly and effectively that you match absolutely everything a buyer wants and rule out everything they might dislike, you might not hear any objections at all. Great. Fantastic. From time to time, great salespeople do skip objections altogether, because their buyer says: 'Right, brilliant, you've met all my needs and there's nothing I need to ask. Let's get straight to the last stage and make a commitment.' But we're here to tell you this doesn't happen very often.

LUCY: Sometimes people will look at a great salesperson and say to themselves: 'That seller doesn't get any objections at all, because they're so good at what they do.' But the truth is, great sellers do get objections. They just don't look like objections because the seller isn't defensive or confrontational. A good seller sees objections for exactly what they are, which is a great opportunity for the salesperson to reassure buyers and explain that you have what they're looking for.

Why It's Natural to Feel Self-Conscious

Let's look at that little word 'objection' that strikes fear into the hearts of many grown salespeople. Do you like the sound of it? Do you relish the prospect of a buyer objecting to what you're offering? No. Why not? Because objections *feel like* conflict, which is what we as human beings tend to avoid at all costs. We don't mean that buyer objections *are* conflict. We just mean that's what they sound like to salespeople. Let's hear a typical objection in a sales situation:

Seller: 'OK, so how does this all look to you so far?'
Buyer: 'No, sorry. It's much too expensive.'

And what does the seller hear?

'I'm rubbish, they hate me, they're never going to buy.'

Especially when you're new to sales, objections sound like there's no way you're going to win a sale now, unless you get stuck into a real battle with the buyer. But in a selling situation, an objection actually *doesn't* necessarily mean conflict.

DAVID: When sellers hear objections, they often think they're hearing 'There's nothing for you here, go and try someone else' and they assume they've blown it. In fact, at the expand stage you'll often feel like you're saying to your buyer: 'So, there you go. You've seen *everything I have to offer... Do you like me?' Which is why objections can feel so terrible, because salespeople feel a buyer is saying: 'No! I don't like you at all.' But objections don't mean game off. They mean, game on, try again. So try again...*

Handling the Big 'O'

We're going to start off by reassuring you that you're perfectly normal if you're a bit apprehensive about buyer objections. We're all built more or less the same, and we have two natural reactions to buyer objections, or perceived conflict: fight or flight. We're sure you've heard these before. Basically, when we imagine there's going to be conflict, the adrenalin starts pumping and we either want to defend ourselves or run away.

As a salesperson, when you hear an objection your natural response is either to want to hang up the phone, or to get really defensive about what you're offering and risk dissolving any rapport you've built up with your buyer. Salespeople are also quite prone to launching into a massive irrelevant presentation when they hear objections and boring their buyer senseless.

And the thing is, these reactions are perfectly normal. So normal, in fact, that it takes practice to educate yourself into taking the third route – the non-conflict route. Great salespeople do two things to overcome their natural reaction to objections:

- They see objections as they really are and know they don't mean 'no sale'.
- They practise dealing with objections without conflict.

So first and foremost, we need to show you objections are a healthy part of the sales process, and certainly don't mean you won't make a sale. Basically, we're going to teach you how to change your perception of objections – and you're going to see objections from the buyer's point of view.

Why Objections Don't Mean It's All Over

Objections happen for two reasons:

- Mismatch: You haven't matched up what you have to offer with what your buyer wants.
- The shall I, shan't I shuffle: Your buyer is thinking things through and making the usual 'buyer noises' before committing.

Neither means a buyer isn't happy with you or won't buy. You're going to learn to breeze through right into the last stage of REPEC: 'commit'.

The Mismatch

Sometimes, despite your best efforts, you'll miss something when exploring or positioning your client and in the expand stage your client will tell you so. They might say something like:

- 'This isn't what I'm looking for.'
- 'No, that part doesn't work for me.'
- 'I like some of what you've said, but not all of it. I don't think it's for me.'

And they're basically telling you to get closer to what they're asking for. This is what we call a mismatch. It means whatever you've said about your product doesn't match what your buyer has said they wanted, and bang! You hit an objection: 'No, that's not what I want, and I don't want to buy it.'

When you've built up rapport, asked questions and positioned your products, mismatch objections are simply a disparity between what your buyer says they want and what you're presenting them as a seller. It doesn't mean your buyer doesn't love you or want what you're offering. And it doesn't mean your buyer is an idiot, who can't see a good thing when it's right in front of them. It just means you need to match things up better.

> DAVID: The expand stage is a bit like being the referee at a football match, talking things through with someone watching the game on TV. People watching football on TV always think the ref is an idiot because the audience can see the whole pitch from loads of different angles. As a salesperson, you don't necessarily have a great view of everything to start off with. And that's why it's so vital to listen to a buyer and not to assume you know what they want. Really good salespeople get far fewer mismatch objections because they listen properly and position everything right. But even the best salespeople miss things here and there, and offer the wrong thing to a buyer from time to time. That's when you get a mismatch objection: basically, your buyer is saying, 'That's wrong, don't want it, don't want to buy it.'

These sorts of objections come about because you, as a salesperson, haven't explained well enough what you're offering in relation to what your buyer wants. Perhaps you haven't explained exactly what you're offering for the money, or your buyer doesn't feel comfortable with everything your product offers. Whatever you haven't explained, your buyer is now saying 'That's not what I want' or 'That's not what I said', and you need to explain things more clearly. Your buyer is really just asking for more information.

If you experience a mismatch, you'll usually need to go right back to exploring your customer better and finding out exactly what they're after. You need to ask in so many words: 'So what do you want to hear that I haven't told you yet?' and 'Is there anything I've said that's turned you off the idea?'

DAVID: When there's a mismatch between what you're showing a buyer and what they want, they may sound a little on the aggressive or defensive side. It's perfectly understandable. After all, if you asked for a fried egg over easy and someone presented you with a soft-boiled egg instead, you might feel a little disappointed and frustrated. So it's really nothing to panic about, and as long as you make sure you carry on finding out exactly what they need, you'll be able to clear up the mismatch easily and get back into the expand stage and check you've got everything right.

The Shall I, Shan't I Shuffle – Avoiding Trodden Toes

The second reason for buyer objections is the 'shall I, shan't I shuffle'. You already know that before buyers commit to something they go through a process which involves weighing up alternatives, thinking about budget, possibly consulting other decision makers etc. We all do it. Think about the last time you purchased something – before you committed to buy you thought through your decision. You said to yourself: 'Shall I, shan't I? Can I afford it? Is it as good as I think it is?' As a buyer, you say: 'I'm not sure, it might be too expensive. I think our current supplier is pretty good…' and so on. These are simply buyer noises. They're the moans and groans we all make before committing to making a purchase, and as long as you don't get into a conflict with your buyer or run away, there's no reason why you can't continue to help them buy your product. The shall I, shan't I shuffle sounds a bit like this:

- 'I need to have a think about it, call me in a few weeks.'
- 'I'm not sure we need to change right now.'
- 'I don't have time to talk at the moment.'

The shall I, shan't I shuffle could take a few moments, or it could take weeks or even months. Be patient, but also be assured that it doesn't mean your buyer doesn't want to buy.

What Buyers Say and What Sellers Hear

What buyers say and what salespeople hear are often worlds apart. Hearing objections as they really are will make the difference between enjoying sales and being great at it, or running away from most buyers with your tail between your legs.

Imagine someone phones you up to invite you on a picnic. They describe a beautiful park with a lake that will make the perfect picnic spot, and explain they've checked the weather forecast and it's going to be a beautiful, sunny day. They talk all about the wonderful food they're going to bring – freshly baked bread, a selection of cheeses, a platter of delicatessen meats…

'That sounds lovely,' you say, 'but I'm a vegetarian.'

How do you think someone would normally respond to that statement? Well, most people would probably say something like: 'OK, we won't do the meat then. But are you happy with everything else?'

But your date says: 'Oh, OK, fine. Sorry to have troubled you.'

Sound ridiculous? It's no more ridiculous than a salesperson hanging up the phone as soon as they hear a buyer objection.

In 'real' life outside sales, if someone puts a barrier in your way you don't immediately throw the whole plan for the day out of the window. You say, 'Come on, let's go for a bit of this. If you don't want to go to the movies with me, what about going for a drink after work?' You should enjoy hearing objections from buyers – they're your opportunity to find out exactly what they want and give you a great opportunity to carry on building rapport.

LUCY: Learning to look at objections differently is very psychological. You've got to control the way you hear these objections so you understand they don't mean someone won't buy. Even if an objection is phrased very aggressively, it isn't meant that way. It isn't an attack on you, it's just 'shall I, shan't I?' You've just got to understand where your buyer is coming from.

As a sales virgin, you won't have a great stock of sales experience behind you to remind yourself just how harmless objections really are, and just how easy it is to work with them to make a sale. So let's examine some typical buyer objections from the buyer's point of view.

Objection!
Buyer: 'It's far too expensive and I really don't think it's worth the money.'

Sellers hear: 'Sorry, I don't like you and I'm not going to buy. Never darken my doorway again.'

But a buyer is really thinking: 'I'm really not sure about the price, and I'm scared about making the wrong decision and losing our company money. I need convincing that this product really will be worth the investment and most of all make me look competent and clever.'

Objection!
Buyer: 'We're not really interested at the moment. Call back in a few weeks.'

Sellers hear: 'They're not interested and they're just try-ing to get rid of me.'

But a buyer is really thinking: 'I'm not confident enough in making this decision and I'm really busy. I need convinc-ing that this opportunity is worth my time at the moment.'

Objection!
Buyer: 'Sorry, we've already got a supplier.'

Sellers hear: 'They have absolutely no need for my prod-uct. I'm wasting my time.'

But a buyer is really thinking: 'I'm very willing to change suppliers, but I need to be convinced that there's a good rea-son to do so.'

Remember: these are *just buying noises*. Buyers are giving you an *opportunity* to sell and have fun with them. Most of all, you're getting the chance to listen once again to what your buyer needs. Our sales team at meta-morphose deal with objections all the time, and they know at first hand they often sound worse than they are. Let's hear what one of our team members has to say about objections:

DAN: Objections aren't about you, and sometimes they're not even about the sale. A buyer could give you a hard time because they've had some bad news that day, or because they've had bad experiences with salespeople before. They could have had ten sales calls that day from really badly trained salespeople, so it's important to really try and understand where someone is coming from when they put forward an objection, and to realise it doesn't mean they don't like you or won't buy.

Part of being able to control the way you hear objections comes down to confidence. The more you hear objections, handle them in the right way and go on to make a sale, the more confident you'll feel that you're simply listening to buyer noises. We'll talk more about ways to boost your confidence in Part III. But for the time being it's really important to remember objections aren't about you. They're the noises a buyer makes when coming to a decision.

LUCY: One of the big mistakes you can make as a salesperson is to take objections personally. A buyer criticises your product for whatever reason and you hear: 'I don't like you.' But objections aren't about you. They're not personal. So don't make them a big deal. Just understand your buyer is asking for more information.

Are you seeing objections a bit more clearly? Let's say it again, just to make it absolutely clear: objections don't mean 'no sale'. Got it? Good. Now you're going to learn the metamorphose step-by-step ACE method of dealing with objections in a non-confrontational way.

How to Be ACE at Handling Objections

At meta-morphose, we've got a formula for dealing with objections called ACE. We should make it very clear that ACE is a learned skill – so it's the opposite of anything natural or innate. There's no such thing as a natural salesperson, and every sales superstar has had to teach themselves at some point how to go against their usual, human impulses. And this is exactly what ACE is going to show you how to do. You're going to learn to deal with objections without conflict, and use good questions to open up the selling situation again and keep everybody communicating well.

If you don't get into a confrontation, you'll absolutely love the part of sales that most people are scared of. Sales *should* be a fun conversation game all the way through, and if you use ACE you'll find objections are a useful and enjoyable part of your job. Listen to what one of our meta-morphose team members has to say about objections – she loves dealing with them!

LISA: I love objections. They're a real challenge and in fact, I think I'd hate to get a call with no objections because they're such a great opportunity to explain exactly why your product is so great. As you probably know, at meta-morphose we send out potential salespeople to be interviewed by our buyers, and part of our job as salespeople is to make sure the candidates we send out match what a buyer has told us they want. From time to time, a buyer doesn't like the candidates we send out and this is often where we have to overcome objections. I received a terrible phone call from a client once, who didn't like the candidate I'd sent. He told me the candidate was awful and that my professional reputation was in tatters. It really wasn't a great thing to hear, but *objections are a good opportunity to find out what clients do want – if you don't take them personally. In the end, I sent him a candidate he absolutely loved and hired for his organisation. So just remember, objections might sound bad but they absolutely don't mean 'no sale'.*

Now let's find out how to be ACE. ACE stands for:

Acknowledge
Clarify
Expand

And it represents three tried-and-tested steps for overcoming objections. We're going to look at each one in turn.

Acknowledge

When you hear a buyer objection, the first thing you have to do is acknowledge it. Show the buyer you've heard them and you understand. This is all about maintaining rapport and listening to what your buyer is telling you to show you're not disagreeing or creating conflict.

> LUCY: I was listening to sales calls for a company on one occasion, and a potential customer told the salesperson that she didn't want to think about renewing her home insurance at the moment as her husband had just died. The salesperson promptly replied: 'Well, you don't want anything else going wrong then, do you?' Talk about not understanding a customer...

The worst thing to do when you hear an objection – and so many salespeople do this – is to immediately tell your buyer how wrong they are. You don't have to agree with your buyer, but you must show them you appreciate their concern is valid – even if you've got a thousand arguments to disprove them. After all, in their world what they're saying *is totally valid*.

LUCY: Not so long ago, I walked into the office of a sales director who immediately said, 'I hate people like you.' I laughed and said, 'Look, in 30 minutes you might be justified in saying that. But right now – wow, what an opening statement. You must have had some terrible experiences with sales companies.' And he said, 'You're right.' All he needed was to have his opinion acknowledged, and after that the conflict was dissolved.

Is your buyer saying your product costs a lot of money? To them, at that moment in time, it *is* a lot of money. There's no point telling them they're wrong and that actually most other companies think your prices are very reasonable.

DAVID: When people are learning how to sell, they often want to know how to handle any and every objection that might be thrown at them, and they want a magic formula. They want to know how the great salespeople they see in action seem to glide through the expand stage without appearing to get any objections at all. Well, if there is a magic formula it's this: don't get confrontational. One of the sweetest things I ever saw in terms of a brilliant salesperson handling objections was watching George – the great seller I told you about earlier – dealing with a customer. He was selling something that had a certain sort of clause or condition to it, and the customer was having none of it. 'No, I won't do it with that condition.' Now, a lot of sellers would see that as a real brick wall. They'd feel they had a real battle on their hands to convince this customer to buy. But George simply said, 'OK. We'll do it your way then.' And straight away there was no conflict. I was astonished, because to me it was a massive obstacle to overcome and for the life of me I couldn't see how these simple words had worked so well. There George was breezing through this major objection and the buyer hardly even blinked. Now of course, with the benefit of experience, I realise George was simply acknowledging the customer's concern without conflict.

Is your buyer telling you they have a current supplier? Of course they have! Not many products today are so original that they've never been thought about in a similar way. Don't think this means 'no sale' – it absolutely doesn't. But you should acknowledge what your buyer is saying and pay attention to their reality. You need to stay calm and in control, and keep everything open and non-confrontational.

LUCY: When you watch a good salesperson in action, you'll be hard pressed to spot at which point a buyer is making an objection, because great sellers simply don't hear objections in the same way most inexperienced or poor sellers do. Sellers who don't see objections as they really are perceive them as confrontation. Great sellers, on the other hand, don't see objections as a problem (which they're not). They recognise them as natural buying habits, and enjoy entering into the game of convincing a buyer that they really are making the right decision. They become curious to find out more about the buyer when they hear an objection. And by being curious, open and non-confrontational, they simply remove any conflict from the situation.

Listen to how one of our meta-sellers stayed non-confrontational and kept the sale on the right track.

RICHARD: I had a meeting in Scotland once with a buyer, and he was quite an academic chap and obviously didn't rate the sales profession too highly. As soon as I arrived, he clearly wanted to take control of the situation and said, 'I'm going to talk, and you're going to listen. I think salespeople talk a load of rubbish...' and so it went on. I sat back and listened, was non-confrontational and acknowledged what he was saying. In the end he calmed down completely and ended up telling me exactly what he wanted without me having to ask. If I'd been defensive and started telling him exactly why salespeople don't talk rubbish, I doubt the meeting would have gone so well.

Clarify

You need to find out exactly what's behind the objection you're hearing. Like all good salespeople, you need to get curious. What does your buyer mean when they say something is too expensive? What are they comparing it to? If they've got a supplier – brilliant! At least they're in the market for what you offer. So you need to question your buyer to really see things from their point of view and get back into their reality. Get into a conversation with them and keep everything open and non-confrontational. Do you remember in the explore stage we talked about open and closed questions? You need to ask open questions to keep your buyer feeding back lots of information to you. For new sellers, it's easy to panic and close down communication by asking closed questions. But you need to keep the dialogue and questioning nice and open.

Expand

You need to give your buyer some really good reasons to buy. You need to outweigh their objection with some really strong, relevant product benefits to show them buying is a great idea. In fact, for every objection you hear, you're going to give two great buying reasons. Then you need to move things forward, hopefully to the 'commit' stage of REPEC by asking them how everything looks. Here are a few good expand phrases to use after you've dealt with an objection:

- How does this sound to you now?
- How does it look now?
- Do you feel more comfortable now?
- Have I explained this?

Our sales team use ACE when they're selling to customers. Here's how one of our sellers has used ACE in the field.

RICHARD: I had a great meeting once with a company, and I sent a few CVs over of some candidates I thought would work well, based on what their buyer had told me he wanted. Then I got a phone message from my buyer telling me he wasn't happy at all, and could I ring him as soon as possible. When I got through to him he told me the candidates' CVs were totally unsuitable for his company and what on earth was I playing at? I told him I totally understood where he was coming from and that what he was saying was right: on paper these candidates perhaps didn't look suitable. I asked him what he found particularly unsuitable about what I'd sent him and he told me they didn't match what he'd asked for. Then I explained that in fact I really had listened to what he wanted and tried to match these candidates accordingly, but this didn't necessarily show itself on paper. I said, 'You asked for two driven, motivated candidates with a "can do" attitude, and this is exactly what I've sent you.' So they both went to interview with him and one of them got the job. You won't overcome every objection, but with ACE you can bring the sale back onto the right footing and create the opportunity to show a buyer exactly how great your product is.

ACE-ing It

Now it's time to look at ACE in action. Let's see some examples of ACE handling some of the most common objections. First of all, we're going to consider a really typical objection: price. This is often an objection new salespeople get panicky about. After all, there's a lot of competition out there, and how do you justify the price of what you're offering if there's something cheaper on the market? Well, first of all don't worry if there are products out there cheaper than yours, because when buyers object to the price of something what they're really talking about is 'value for money'. Your buyer might say they want the cheapest thing going, but if the cheapest thing doesn't give them what they need it's not good value. So you need to make sure that whatever price your product is, you can communicate its value to buyers. Let's take a look at ACE dealing with a price objection:

Buyer: 'Thanks, but I can get it cheaper elsewhere.'

Acknowledge: 'Fine, I understand you need good value for money, and there are others out there offering what we offer. But if you just give me a minute I'll explain how we can give you value for money.

Clarify: What does value mean for you? What are you comparing us to? What specifically do you find expensive? What would have to be in place for you to feel you were getting good value for money?'

Buyer: 'I'd have to save around 25% of my current spend on this sort of service.'

Expand: 'Let me explain in more detail how I believe we can make these savings for you:

Reposition two product benefits:

Our product actually lasts around twice as long as the one you're currently using, which means that you're getting 50% more for only a 10% higher price.

Also, we offer a free service contract, which means you'll save £xx this year alone.

And move things forward...

How does this sound to you now?'

You can talk about how your product offers value in comparison to others out there, but you shouldn't slate the competition. If you've got a good product it's unnecessary anyway, and it's not professional to do down other providers in the market. Having said that, you do need to be able to explain exactly why someone should buy from you instead of a competitor. So if your product is more expensive than someone else's, you should be able to explain this price difference and what you offer for the extra money. After all, everyone would buy the cheapest product if there's no good reason to buy a more expensive one.

If someone says they're thinking about a lower-priced competitor, you should ideally be able to explain the difference between your product and the cheaper version. You might say something like:

'The less expensive product you're talking about is an off-the-shelf solution, which is great if you want a cheap, quick fix and don't need anything tailored to your business. However, because you've told me your business is quite unique, I'd suggest you need something more along the lines of what we offer. We cost more, but for that extra price you get a lot of extra value. This is what we do. We offer...'

What you don't want to say is: 'You don't want an off-the-shelf solution, they're a load of rubbish. Six months down the line when it all falls apart you'll wish you'd listened to me!'

DAVID: Like all premium-priced business services, meta-morphose has competition: other companies offer what appears to be a similar service to us. So it's vital for our sales team to be able to explain just what the difference is between us and other providers. We always have the facts and figures to hand to prove the results we offer, including success stories over ten years to prove companies get good value for money and a great return on their investment. Don't worry if your product isn't the cheapest out there. Just make sure you can prove why buyers should choose you over the competition.

Above all, you should be honest when communicating value, and remember to carry on acknowledging your buyer's viewpoint. If your product is at the top of the price scale, it's OK to say: 'Yes, we're one of the more high-end products out there, but what we offer gives you much more value.'

DOING IT: Make a note of the average cost to the buyer of what you sell here:

£

Think about the value your product offers buyers for the price they pay for it. Really think about the price they pay, versus the time saving, cost saving or other advantages your product offers. Consider the materials your product is made from, or the trained staff who are involved with the service you're offering. Think about the value it will add to your buyer's organisation. Now write down three reasons why your product justifies its price tag:

1
2
3

Find a competitor who offers a lower-priced version of your service and write down the average sale price:

£

Write a brief description of your competitor's product, using simple words and phrases to quickly explain how it's different from what you offer.

Now write down the extra things your product offers and explain why it's worth a higher price:

If there are no competitors offering a cheaper version of what you do, you might want to write down exactly why your lower-priced product offers customers better value than the competition:

Not Tonight – I'm Washing My Hair...

Let's move onto another common objection: 'I can't deal with this right now, so phone me back or send me something.' It basically means: 'I can't be bothered to make any changes.' Many businesses survive because people can't be bothered to change. In fact, the first bank to offer phone banking – which basically gave customers a flexible and better service – had a terrible time trying to get people to switch even though it had something really new and innovative to offer buyers. Your job as a salesperson is to make everything as easy as possible for customers. You should make it easier for them to buy than to refuse. Let's see how ACE handles this sort of objection:

Buyer: 'Send me some information.'
Acknowledge: 'OK, no problem.
Clarify: What sort of information would you like?'
Buyer: 'I don't know – just the usual stuff.'

LUCY: At this point you might feel like giving up and just sending some general information. Don't. You need to find out if you offer what these people need, or else you're wasting everyone's time. Value your time as a salesperson - you'll make much more money! So keep everything nice and open, and carry on clarifying by asking questions to find out what your buyer needs...

Clarify: 'What sort of information would convince you that our product is a good idea?'

Buyer: 'I'd have to see something that would definitely add value to our business.'

Expand: 'OK. Well, if you'll give me a moment I think I can explain how our product can add value:

Reposition two product benefits

Our product is much simpler to use than others on the market, which means that your staff will have more time to add value to your business.

It will also make what you offer look more attractive, which means that you're likely to sell more and make more profit.

And move things forward

How does this sound to you now?'

Let's look at how ACE deals with another common objection along these lines:

Buyer: 'OK, we'll think about it... call me back in a few weeks.'

Acknowledge: 'I understand you're busy.

Clarify: What would I have to say to make this call worth your while right now?'

Buyer: 'Well, you'd have to tell me what you're offering is totally free.'

Expand: 'OK, well let me explain what is free about what we offer:

Reposition two product benefits

Our product comes with a free warranty, which means that you'll receive free service and repair for 12 months. You'll also be able to contact our customer services free of charge, which means any operational questions you have will be answered quickly and easily.

And move things forward

Do you feel more comfortable now?'

I'm Having an Affair...

Now let's look at an objection you're bound to run into if you're contacting the right buyers: 'We've already got someone selling us what you offer.' Sellers often find this a devastating objection. How could you? Don't I mean anything to you? But as we've already mentioned, there's no reason to think someone won't buy just because they've already got a supplier. And it means they're definitely in the market for what you're offering.

Buyer: 'We've got a current supplier...'

Acknowledge: 'I appreciate you've got a current supplier, but I think I can explain how we can offer you better value.

Clarify: What do you really like about your current supplier?'

Buyer: 'I know what I'm getting. We've used them for years.'

Expand: 'That's great. I'm glad you've got a good relationship with your suppliers.

Reposition with two product benefits
We're actually noted for our strong relationships with customers, which means that you get really reliable, friendly service with our company. In fact, xx company has told us recently they use us because of our good customer service.
Also, we work with some really big names in your field, which means we have a proven track record as a trustworthy supplier.
And move things forward
How do we sound to you now?'

I'm Just Not Attracted to You
Finally, we're going to look at how ACE handles a buyer who doesn't like your company.

Buyer: 'Your company is awful – I've heard terrible things about your customer service.'
Acknowledge: 'I apologise for that. I'm sorry you've heard bad things about us.
Clarify: How can we help change that impression? What do we have to do to start again?'
Buyer: 'You'd have to prove to me that your customer service is very good.'
Expand: 'We have needed to improve in the past.
Reposition with two product benefits
But I can tell you we've hired lots more staff for our customer service team in the last year, which means that now you'll always get fast service when you need it.
Also, we offer dedicated customer service for business, which means that we're now one of the most accessible companies for people like you.

And move things forward
How do you feel about us now?'

DOING IT: We've got a great game we play at meta-
morphose to get our sales virgins practising handling objections in the real world. When you're selling you have to deal
with objections fast, so what we do is stand our trainees
around in a circle, shout out an objection and chuck a ball
at one of them. Whoever we've aimed the ball at has to
catch it, then put the ACE formula into action. You're going
to do a version of that game yourself to get you in good
shape for sales. We're going to give you a list of typical
objections and we'd like you to write them on bits of paper
and drop them into a hat. Here they are:

Someone else is cheaper.
I'm not interested.
I've already been told by others in my organisation that
we don't need this product/service.
Your company is terrible.
I don't have the time.
We've got a current supplier.
We'll think about it.
We'd like to change but it's too much hassle.

Now simply pull one out of a hat at random and give
ACE a go. Try to practise at least three times with each
one – or until you're comfortable answering it quickly.
You'll be surprised how difficult it is at first to answer
quickly on the spot, but by the third time you might be
equally surprised by how easy you find it!

An Answer for Everything

Sometimes when a buyer makes an objection, they're asking for something you really can't deliver. New sellers often find this difficult, because they feel as a good salesperson you should be able to meet all a buyer's needs or you'll lose the sale. But this isn't true. Listen to the following objection:

'No, that's too expensive. I'd like a brand new computer for around the £10 mark. And can you throw in a fax machine too?'

Do you think you need to offer the buyer exactly what they've asked for to make a sale? Of course not. You don't need to have an answer for everything. You just have to go back to exploring your buyer, and finding out exactly what they'd be happy with if they can't have it all. Or finding a compromise in terms of cost and re-positioning your product accordingly.

DAVID: Sometimes, a client will phone us up to ask for a salesperson. And they'll say something like: 'We need someone familiar with engineering who speaks fluent Cantonese, lives in Scotland and is willing to travel to China.' Now that's a difficult call. And we can't necessarily give them exactly what they want at that moment in time, so you have to be honest about it. But if someone wants something really obscure, the chances are they haven't had a lot of luck finding it in the past, so any help you're offering in solving their problem will be gratefully received. In a tricky situation, we might say something like: 'We don't have someone available, but we'll write the ads, hunt for the person you're looking for and do everything we can to help.' You don't have to meet all of a client's needs for them to buy. But you do have to understand what they need, and just be honest about what you can and can't offer.

Walking Away

Just like dating, you won't be right for everybody and at times you'll just have to walk away. And it's usually in the expand stage were you have to make this decision. If you can't match what the buyer wants, be honest. Explain that you don't offer exactly what they're after and suggest what you can do that might work instead – but be prepared to walk away if you genuinely can't meet their needs. You'll have your reputation and ethics intact, and in the long run you'll win more business. Listen to what two of our meta-morphose team members say about walking away.

RICHARD: Often salespeople think you always have to fight to make your buyer interested, and always make sure they're the one to walk away. But a better way to look at it is to value your time, and only spend as long with a buyer as is worthwhile. Ask yourself, is it worth spending a long time with one person who doesn't really have a need for your product, when you could be making really good connections with other people who do? With experience, you're able to judge a sales situation quickly, and decide the right time to leave a sale and move on to the next one if needs be.

LISA: A really common objection is about price, and there is a level where you have to walk away. You can only go down to a certain price, and if a buyer wants you to back down more than is feasible you have to say: 'Sorry, we're not right for you at this moment in time. Thanks very much for the opportunity to discuss things and maybe we can work together in the future.' And more often than not, you will work with them in the future, when they realise your product really is worth the money.

Walking away doesn't mean you've failed or there's something wrong with what you're offering. It just means it's not right for that particular buyer at that moment in time, but you can always try again in the future.

DAVID: Years ago I worked for a London publishing company which sold coffee-table books and art for the masses. We did a big line in posters - the sort of thing you see rolled up in bins in Athena. I used to sell Aubrey Beardsley prints, which are Art Nouveau-style black-and-white art, and if you were around in the 1970s you'd know that almost every student at every university had an Aubrey Beardsley print hanging on their bedroom wall. I spent many happy years in that industry, and at the time we were offering something really unique by bringing 'tasteful' art to greeting cards and posters. Anyway, do you remember the poster of the girl tennis player scratching her bum? I rejected that poster for our company. A man came up to me while we had a stand in Birmingham and he had half a dozen to sell. I looked at them and said: 'Cor, they're bloody great, but they're not our thing. We're a bit more artsy fartsy.' I sent him over to Athena and that poster became the best-selling poster ever printed. Now I'm not saying I was wrong to turn him away - after all, his poster wasn't right for us. But what I'm saying is sometimes your product won't be right for a buyer, no matter how fantastic it is. And as an honest salesperson sometimes you have to be the one to walk away. If you can genuinely see what you're offering isn't right for a buyer, don't try to sell it to them. The quicker you establish this and let go, the quicker you'll find a buyer who is truly right for what you're offering.

How do you know when to walk away? You'll just have to practise selling and listen to your instincts. However, hopefully you're not walking away from the sale just yet, so you're ready to learn about the fifth and final stage of REPEC: 'commit'.

11

Commit – Asking for What You Want

So now you're at the final stage of REPEC: 'commit'. To finish the sale, you need to ask your customer to commit to what you're offering. This is also referred to as 'closing' a sale, and it's the part where you ask for the business, wrap everything up for your customer and give them their product. And we're going to give you the confidence and the skills to help your buyers commit quickly and easily, so you'll be beating your sales targets in no time. You're just one step away from winning the sale, making a nice amount of commission and giving your buyer a great product.

Don't You Want Me? Rejection Made Easy

Before we tell you exactly how to close a sale, or ask buyers to commit, we're going to put to rest some of the fears you might have about rejection. Commit is probably the simplest and quickest stage of selling, and yet people with fantastic sales potential often stop short here and waste all the good work they've put in so far. Why? Well, we've told you sometimes you have to walk away from a sale if you don't think your product matches your customer's needs. But sometimes your customer will tell *you* they're not interested. Despite your brilliant rapport and fantastic listening skills and great positioning, a customer might still say no.

Even the best salespeople have buyers turning them down, or experience rejection. We've found that sales virgins are often terrified the commit stage will be the part when buyers tell them to take a hike, and sometimes fear of rejection stops sellers going through the commit stage altogether. Every other stage of REPEC may have gone brilliantly, yet instead of moving to the final stage we watch many a new seller walk themselves back into a sale instead of closing and winning the business. It's quite a common thing for sales virgins to avoid commitment. After all, in the commit stage you're asking your buyer to buy – and if you don't ask for something, you won't get rejected, right?

DAVID: I've met brilliant salespeople who've got great rapport and work through all the REPEC stages perfectly, but who say at the last minute 'I expect you want to think about it?' because they don't want to ask for something and get rejected. This is a total no-no if you want to sell, but fear of rejection is a very common thing. It can totally paralyse brilliant sellers, even when it's quite clear their customer is just waiting to be asked.

It's probably fear of rejection that stops a lot of people going into sales in the first place, and feeds the stereotype that salespeople always have 'something to prove'. After all, surely most *normal* people wouldn't put themselves in line for rejection day after day? You've probably heard it yourself – 'I couldn't do sales, I'm not good at taking rejection.'

We're going to give you the confidence to ask for business, so you can make sure you're winning all the sales you can. We're here to tell you you've got nothing to fear from asking for commitment and we promise you're not going to have your heart broken when you ask buyers to buy.

Recognise Me!

Are salespeople simply better at dealing with rejection than other people? No. As a matter of fact, people who go into sales are likely to have a higher fear of rejection than the next person, so if you're apprehensive about the idea of closing a sale, this shows you've probably got just the character necessary to be a salesperson.

> DAVID: People often say that good salespeople are good at handling rejection. But the truth is, really good salespeople are probably even more likely to dislike being rejected, because they're the sort of people who want to get on with everyone.

Remember we talked in Part I about our need to be recognised? Well, now we come to an interesting point about good salespeople. We all crave certain levels of recognition at one time or another, but outstanding salespeople tend to have what we at meta-morphose call 'high recognition trait'. What we mean by this is they want to be recognised more than most people. They want to stand out. Most people want at least one person to like them, and they want to be recognised some of the time. But people with high recognition trait want *lots* of people to like them, notice and accept them *all* the time.

The sales trainees we meet at meta-morphose usually have high recognition trait, and you probably do too. How do we know? Because you have the ambition and drive to read a book telling you how to excel at sales.

> DAVID: Great salespeople usually can't live on a level of simply being accepted by one other person. They need to be accepted and noticed by lots of people or they

wouldn't go into the sales profession in the first place, which is after all an industry built on being recognised for meeting targets. People with high recognition trait aren't show-offs, or arrogant or anything like that. They're usually very eager to please, which is one of the things that makes a great salesperson. But it also means they hate the idea of being rejected: hence they sometimes have trouble getting into the commit stage of selling. The good news is, the commit stage isn't really about acceptance and rejection.

Ask yourself the following:

- Do you often do things other people wouldn't bother doing?
- Do you choose clothes that make you stand out?
- Is it very important for you to be liked by everyone you meet?

If you answered yes to any or all of these questions, you've probably got just the qualities necessary to be a really great salesperson. But there's a catch. It doesn't take a genius to work out that if you want people to like you, rejection is certainly *not* what you want. So we're well aware that people with the characteristics to do really well in sales are often afraid of rejection when asking people for commitment. We work hard at meta-morphose to make sure our trainees go into the commit stage of REPEC with as much confidence as all the other stages. And before you ask for commitment, we're going to make absolutely sure you know there's really nothing to be afraid of.

Why You Don't Close Business

Fear of rejection is why sellers – especially sales virgins – don't close business. Asking for commitment is often the BIG FEAR for sales virgins. But you've got to get it in perspective. It's only finishing up the sale. The most important thing to remember is if you've carried out REPEC properly, it's highly unlikely you'll be rejected. If your product isn't right for a buyer, you'll have discovered this in the earlier stages and walked away from the sale. Good sellers find out their products aren't right *before* customers do, so if the sale is going right you'll be the one choosing whether to move on or not.

If your product *is* right, the worst anyone is going to say is 'I'm not ready to commit right now' – so try again later. But even so, sales virgins often have a real fear of asking for commitment. They worry that the buyer won't like them any more if they ask for business and the buyer says it's not the right time. Or they feel they'll sound pushy or rude by asking outright. But it's really silly to think you can't be friends with a buyer if they're not ready to commit right away. Our sales team at meta-morphose are great friends with a number of potential buyers who've never made a commitment, but are happy to have a chat now and again about their needs.

RICHARD: People say salespeople get rejected all the time, day in and day out. But I don't think they do. If I were to spend months and months building a relationship with a customer, only for them to tell me at the end of it all that they weren't going to buy because they didn't like me and furthermore I smelt bad – that would be rejection. But when I talk to a new buyer and they tell me they don't want to commit to my product at that moment in time, this really isn't anything to take personally. If what you're selling is perfect for them it can feel frustrating, but just be patient and try again in a few months' time.

And it's not pushy or rude to ask buyers for their business: if you've followed REPEC properly, buyers will be confused if you *don't* ask. What's really so hard about asking for commitment? What's the worst thing that could happen? If your buyer doesn't want to commit right now, that doesn't mean you've failed. They just haven't committed at that moment in time. They still might in the future, and there are still loads of people out there who will want to commit. You've just got to take the bull by the horns and go for it. Asking is all that's standing between you and the sale.

> DOING IT: Remember a time when you asked for something and someone happily gave it to you. This could be a family member, friend, whoever. Choose a situation where you were asking for something perfectly reasonable – something you wouldn't usually think twice about. It should also be an occasion where you felt very happy and accepted. Now try to picture exactly where you were standing or sitting, the posture you adopted and the words you used. Picture the other person and remember how they sounded and what they said. Try to remember the exact details of the setting, such as floor colour, furniture, temperature and smell. Really get into the scene and picture yourself there. Feel how you felt at the time. This is a hugely effective technique for changing your mood and feelings, and if you're ever scared about being rejected, you can call on this memory and instantly evoke the feelings of being comfortable and happy asking for what you want.

We're going to give you more confidence-boosting ideas in Part III. But now, let's find out exactly what to do to win commitment.

The Key Words that Win a Sale – and Those that Don't

So what are the 'magic' words that win a sale? There are none. You don't need to make a big deal of asking for commitment: you've already done all the hard work. All you need to do is ask for the business.

LUCY: How do you get commitment? Just ask for it. I have an exercise I do with my trainees, where I get them all sitting in a circle. And I walk around and say, 'Can I have your watch?' And whoever I've asked will give me their watch. And then I say to another trainee, 'Can I have your shoe?' And they'll take off their shoe and give it to me. I do this all around the circle, asking for various things, and then I explain myself: 'If you don't ask, you don't get!' If you've done a good job, asked great questions and given your buyer exactly what they wanted, there's no reason at all why you shouldn't ask for the business.

Yet many new sellers get to the commitment stage and say something like:

'So this is everything. But perhaps you wouldn't like it now. I'll leave you to think about it.'

Or:

'OK, so that all sounds good to you. And the price is right. So tell me more about yourself...'

And all sorts of variations, just to get out of *asking* for the business. And they go walking back into the sale, even though they're just a few words away from securing the business.

LUCY: You're taught your whole life to wait until you're offered, not to ask outright. It's habitual and a very British thing. We don't like asking for business. I've trained about 9,000 salespeople and they can be brilliant right until they get to the commit stage. Then they lose it and come out with things like: 'Actually, ...you'll find it will cost about... and if that sounds too much.... And I'll go back and talk things over...' People instinctively avoid asking for things because it's all a little bit rude. I've seen people get to commit and then walk back into the sale. Or they'll say: 'Would you like to go ahead... but of course if you don't want to right now.' Because they're scared. But this is very easy to educate yourself out of.

Many people see great sellers close business, or ask buyers to commit, and think: 'That seller has some sort of magic formula for closing a sale.' People think that if you say the right words, a buyer will fall to their knees and buy anything. But the only magic of commit is in the previous stages of REPEC. When buyers don't commit, it's usually not because you phrased things wrong or didn't get your tone of voice right. If a buyer won't commit, you were almost certainly never in a position to ask them for their business in the first place.

LUCY: When you ask for commitment, you're really going to find out if you carried out each stage of REPEC properly. Because if you didn't ask the right questions, didn't find out your buyer's solution, didn't find out there were other decision makers... whatever it is you didn't do, you're going to find out all about it when you ask your buyer to commit.

There are a few different ways you can ask for commitment, so let's take a look at your choices. Here are four types of closing question you can use:

1. Assumptive questions
2. Recommendation questions
3. Direct questions
4. Alternative questions

The easiest way to explain these questions is to give you examples of them. Since you're a sales virgin, we're going to give you dating versions of these questions so you can see them in action:

Assumptive: Let's go back to my place.
Recommendation: I'd recommend we go to my place – it's much nearer.
Direct: Would you like to come back to mine?

And the all-time classic:

Alternative: Your place or mine?

DAVID: The commit stage is basically asking 'Where do we go from here?' and anyone can do it. I was always taught to go with the alternative close 'Do you want that in red or white?' because people's minds cope better with alternatives than decisions. The alternative close probably works better if you're not feeling that brave, but it's just as easy to say 'When would you like it?' As long as you've followed REPEC, it's not rude or pushy to ask with the assumption your buyer is going to buy.

DOING IT: How are you going to ask for the business? Work out your own four closes based on the above four techniques:

1. Assumptive close

2. Recommendation close

3. Direct close

4. Alternative close

LUCY: 99% of the time, I use the recommendation close. I'll say something like: 'Based on everything you've said, this is what I suggest we do.' This is generally the close I suggest salespeople use, although it's totally the choice of the individual seller. When you're a bit more experienced, you can also try putting the control back into the hands of the buyer, by saying: 'What do you suggest we do next?' I wouldn't recommend it for new salespeople and I think it would worry a lot of sales managers – but when you've got a few sales under your belt, feel free to give it a go.

Sometimes, you won't have to close because your buyer will close for you. You'll have done such a fantastic job, they'll say, 'OK, sounds great. Where do I sign?' and you're away.

DAVID: If customers think they're going to miss the boat, they'll often fall over themselves to commit to your product. One of the things that drives people in terms of motivation is thinking they can't have something. In sales, there's something called 'negative selling', which basically means showing someone something and then gradually pulling it away from them so they feel inclined to chase after it. You see negative selling all over the place: 'Last days of sale!' 'Hurry! While stocks last!' If you've got an exclusive product, you might be lucky enough to have a buyer chasing you for commitment rather than the other way around.

The Right Time to Pop the Question

If you've followed every other stage of REPEC properly, the commit stage will be a walk in the park. If you haven't, then you're not in any position to close and any questions you didn't ask or facts you should have discovered will come back to haunt you.

How do you know when to ask for commitment? When you've followed REPEC thoroughly, dealt with buyer objections and re-positioned everything so everyone is happy, then you'll almost certainly be at the right stage to ask for commitment. But don't forget to use your instincts. You'll have a feeling of the right time to ask, and also if it's too soon.

There's nothing worse than a seller asking for the business before a buyer is ready: it exerts a lot of pressure, and customers may just decide to forget the whole idea entirely for that reason, and that reason alone.

> DAVID: A word of advice. Make sure you settle all concerns about price before asking for commitment. You'll often find buyers will say everything is OK, but you have to talk about the price. When your buyer has agreed to everything, you've shown them a model which gives them what they want and you both agree the price is right – that's the time to ask for the business.

Sometimes – especially when you're a sales virgin – you'll ask for commitment too soon and hear a lot of objections, which means you need to go back into the sale and start asking questions again. Don't worry too much about this. You can still win the sale: just get curious about your buyer again and find out exactly what it is you haven't matched up properly yet.

> LUCY: If a buyer is scared of commitment, use ACE again and go back into the sale. You should never go over the top about closing. A lot of sales managers ask me to come in and teach their team how to ask for commitment. What I can guarantee is that closing isn't the problem. If your buyer doesn't want to commit, it's usually because you haven't asked the right questions and you weren't in the right position to close. So get back into the sale, ask more questions and try again.

What are their misgivings? What haven't you explained properly? Get some good, honest dialogue going again until you feel you're in a position to close.

And If They Still Say No...

Sometimes your product will be totally perfect for a buyer, they'll have the right budget, you've answered all their concerns and they still don't want to commit. If you feel you've done your best in a sale, move on – making a note to contact that buyer again in the next six months. Our sellers walk away from sales every day, at least in the short term, without sobbing into their pillows at night. They haven't failed or been rejected. On the contrary, they've freed up valuable time to get to know even more buyers.

Buyer's Remorse and Why You'll Avoid It

Buyer's remorse happens when you make a purchase but regret it almost as soon as you've committed to buy. You look at the flashy new computer you've just bought and think: 'Actually, do I really need something so expensive?' For whatever reason, what you were promised doesn't match up to the reality and you feel disappointed. If there's a salesperson involved you're unlikely to feel very warm towards them or inclined to purchase from them again in the future.

> DAVID: One of the things I stipulate at meta-morphose is that when the deal is done the customer must feel good. There's something called buyer's remorse, which we all get when we realise we don't want something. It's that unpleasant feeling that you're saddled with something that doesn't really meet your needs. If a customer feels that when they're spending a lot of money, you won't do business with them again.

Buyer's remorse occurs for two (often combined) reasons:

1. A seller hasn't been honest about what their product offers, or concerned with a buyer's genuine needs.
2. As soon as the sale is made, the seller is out of the door and onto the next buyer without offering any support or aftercare.

If someone doesn't feel happy when they've made a purchase, not only are they not going to buy from you again, but they're not going to recommend you to anyone else – and word-of-mouth recommendations are an incredibly important part of sales. This is especially true in the business world where people make very large purchases and a lot of egos are on the line. So it's important your buyer feels good after they've bought your product.

With meta-selling, you'll largely avoid buyer's remorse because you'll have been totally honest and open about your product, and willing to walk away if you can't meet your buyer's needs. But you should also remember that 'commit' isn't the end of the sale. It's the beginning of a long and beneficial relationship between you and the buyer. Winning a sale is really exciting (we told you selling is fun), but don't get so caught up in the moment that you forget all about your customer. When your buyer has signed on the dotted line, it's vital you take responsibility for ensuring they receive absolutely everything you've promised them. Don't rush out of the door assuming your job is over. It isn't. Make sure your customer feels good and looked after, and above all ensure you deliver exactly what you've said you will.

12

REPEC for the Telephone

Most business sellers phone up buyers they've never met before as part of the sales process. This is called 'cold calling', and we often hear people say: 'I hate cold calling, it's so pushy. I could never do it.' The idea of phoning up total strangers might sound a bit daunting if you've never done it before, but if you learn to do it the meta-morphose way it's enjoyable and a great way to meet buyers. You'll really enjoy calling up potential customers, or 'prospecting' as we sometimes call it. REPEC is designed to be used both during face-to-face sales and over the telephone. However, there are some specific things that are helpful to learn about selling by phone, and we're going to fill you in on them right now. There's really nothing more natural than contacting people by telephone to let them know about a product that could interest them. And it's also lots of fun.

> LUCY: I love cold calling. Whether or not you enjoy it really comes down to your attitude: if you approach cold calling as something unpleasant it's more than likely that's the experience you'll have. But if you think to yourself, 'I'm going to ring a few people, have some interesting conversations and make a few sales', that's exactly what will happen. As long as you give people a good reason to talk to you, you'll really enjoy yourself.

Some people are masters of the telephone almost immediately, and others need a little more practice. The telephone is an interesting way to sell, because both you and your buyer are deprived of one of your senses: sight. Without being able to see your buyer, you won't be able to pick up visual clues from their gestures and expressions about whether you're hitting the spot. But you'll become very good at working out how your buyer is feeling over the telephone from signals and clues in their voice. If you think that sounds unlikely, think about what you pick up when you talk to family or friends over the telephone. We bet you can tell instantly what sort of mood they're in within a few seconds of the call. Great sellers can do this with anyone, and just like any other skill it just comes down to trying it out and learning as you go along.

DAVID: We had a lady who worked in our sales team years ago, and she was an absolute natural on the telephone. She had a real gift for picking up clues from people's voices about how they were feeling. Her rapport was so good that people used to come to the office and want to meet her - but she was so shy about face-to-face contact we sometimes had to drag her out kicking and screaming! She was so good at selling over the phone that she won the National Sales Awards - which just goes to show what a big part cold calling plays in selling. You might have a natural gift for the telephone too, but if you find it hard at first don't worry. The more you practise communicating, the better you'll get.

DOING IT: The next time you phone up someone you know well, pay attention to their voice and try to pinpoint exactly what lets you know how they're feeling. Does the tone of their voice go up if they're feeling excited? Or down? Do they talk more quickly if they're pleased about something, or does their voice slow down? Make notes about what you learn:

Remember our diagram in Chapter 7 about first impressions? How people judge you in the first few seconds of meeting you is largely based on how you look. Over the telephone, of course, people can only judge you on how you sound and what you're saying. If you've got a naturally pleasant voice, lucky you, but more important are your tone and manner. It's important your voice is calm, confident and trustworthy when you're speaking to buyers, and in order to make sure that's the case you need to be totally prepared for the call.

> DOING IT: Ring up a company offering a similar product to yours, but who isn't a direct competitor, and talk to someone there about their services. Ask questions and find out all you can about what they're offering – you may even pick up some good ideas about how to present your own product. When you've finished, thank them for their time.
>
> Notice throughout the call how calm and confident you sound. You'll find confidence comes very easily when you're on the buying side of things. So ask yourself, why shouldn't you sound exactly the same as a seller? After all, you're a business professional with something important to discuss with your buyer.

Winning Telephone Sales with REPEC

We're going to look at REPEC again now – this time giving you a bit more advice about exactly how to use it when you're cold calling.

Rapid Rapport

First of all, let's look at generating rapport over the telephone. The main thing to remember is you do everything more quickly when you're cold calling. You have to generate rapport in seconds, and you're going to do that with a great opening line and by using the chat-up line you created in Chapter 7. An opening line is simply what you say when you first get through to someone on the phone. After all, it's polite to quickly introduce yourself before you get down to business. You're going to design your own opening line right now. It should be no more than five seconds long, and be totally genuine and honest. Here are a few examples we use at meta-morphose:

'Hello. My name's Lucy and I'm calling from a company called meta-morphose. This is the first time we've spoken. Do you have a moment to talk?'

'Hi _____. I'm David from meta-morphose. I'm sorry to interrupt you. Do you mind if I ask, who usually handles your training there?'

DOING IT: What are you going to say when you first get through to someone on the phone? We'll leave you to be creative here, but whatever you say must be sincere, polite and last no more than five seconds when spoken out loud. Make a note of your opening line here:

Remember in Chapter 7 when we talked about chat-up lines? On the telephone, chat-up lines are how you build rapport. You need to give people a great reason for your call within a few seconds, and if you manage to do that your buyer will be interested – at least for the moment – in hearing what you have to say. We've said it before and we'll say it again: your buyer will *always* be doing something more important when you ring up, so you must give them a great reason to talk to you – and fast.

> DOING IT: Hit us with your chat-up line right now, without referring back to your notes. Say it out loud, clearly and as smoothly as possible. Can you do it? If so, well done. You've got just the sort of motivation and attitude we look for in our meta-sellers. If not, go back and learn it right now. You *should* know it totally off by heart.

Always Explore

As soon as you've got your buyer's attention, you need to move immediately into 'explore' to get them talking about themselves. It's common for telephone sellers to launch into a 'mini sale' (i.e. positioning) the second a buyer picks up the phone, and it can feel very tempting to do this if you can sense your customer is busy. But don't. How would you feel if you sat down in a restaurant, only to be presented with a meal your date had pre-ordered you? Remember, you don't have permission to position your product until you've asked your buyer all about them. So always ask questions before you talk about yourself.

Prompt Positioning

Now you've got all the information you need, you can present your product but do it quickly. It's even more important over the telephone to keep your presentation as succinct as possible, so respect your buyer's time and do just that by keeping benefits to a minimum. The more calls you make, the better you'll get at working out whether you're hitting the spot without being able to see your buyer's expression.

Expand Efficiently...

Here are some objections you're more likely to hear over the phone:

1. You're the 10th salesperson to call me this week.
2. I'm happy with my current supplier.
3. You're too expensive, my budget is really tight.
4. I don't have time for a meeting.
5. Send me some information in the post.
6. I'll call you if I'm interested.

...But Handle Commit Differently

Because you go through REPEC over the telephone much faster than you would during a face-to-face sale, you're not necessarily expecting your buyer to commit straight away. They may do, but then again you may not even get to speak to your potential buyer the first time you call a company. But you should always get a commitment in some form, and make sure you move the situation forward positively. So if you don't get to speak to your buyer, try to find out their full name, the time they're likely to be in and get permission to phone back again to speak to them. Or if your buyer asks you to send in literature, make sure you find out exactly what they're likely to need, and ask them what your next move should be when they receive it. Make sure at the end of every call you've gained something that's moved you towards a sale – or at the very least found out more about the needs of a company. You should be the one specifying the terms of the commitment. If a buyer says 'Call back', you need to find out the right time to call and make sure whoever you're talking to agrees. Feel free to use assumptive language when you're closing, such as 'What you'll find working with us...' or 'When I next speak to you...' It helps put the sale on a positive footing and moving forward.

> LUCY: At the end of every call you should feel good. You should also feel like you've made some progress. So even if you don't win an order, you should feel brilliant if you've got some information or agreed a good time to call back. If you don't get some sort of commitment, you won't believe you've moved forward and the call will feel like a waste of time – which will sap your motivation.

The Telesales Ladder – and Why *Everyone* Counts

OK. So the truth is when you're phoning a company you really want to speak to someone who can make a buying decision straight away. But more commonly you'll start off speaking to a receptionist, and it's up to them to put you through to whoever makes the buying decisions. Sellers make a big mistake when they treat people who answer the phone as 'gatekeepers' or 'minions', and try to 'get past them' to speak with a buyer. Everyone you speak to is a human being who deserves equal respect, and by being polite, open and honest with everyone you're much more likely to get the right result. If you were meeting a date at their family home for dinner, you'd be polite and friendly to any of their family and friends you met. Think of all company employees as friends and family of your buyer and make sure you're polite and courteous to them too.

When you speak to a PA or office manager, you might experience objections right up front before you've even talked about your product. Here are some typical objections:

1. What's it concerning?
2. Is he or she expecting your call?
3. Is it a sales call?
4. Can I help you with that?
5. He or she won't be in for a few weeks/months.
6. Just send something in the post.

Because these objections aren't coming from a buyer, it's easy for sellers to forget about ACE and get into conflict. But you should deal with these objections in the same way you would during a sale. Acknowledge the point of view of whoever you're talking to, and find out more. The first two stages are the most important here. Let's look at an example:

Call Answerer: 'Can you send us some written information?'
Acknowledge: 'I can do that for you. We do have a lot of different information here.
Clarify: So, what specific information would be useful?'

Call Answerer: 'Can I help you with that?'
Acknowledge: 'Yes, certainly.
Clarify: What specifically would you like to know about us first?'

Call Answerer: 'The person you need to speak to is in a meeting.'
Acknowledge: 'Sure.
Clarify: When will they be free?'
And you can also try:
'What is a good time to get hold of this person?'
'How do you suggest I get hold of this person? Should I email? Or would phoning be better?'

DOING IT: Can you guess what we're going to ask you to do next? That's right: think about how you're going to answer the remaining five objections above using the ACE formula. Off you go:

1. Acknowledge

    Clarify

    Explain

2. Acknowledge

    Clarify

    Explain

3. Acknowledge

    Clarify

    Explain

DAVID: With meta-selling, no one is a minion. Everyone is a human being, and worth talking to and getting to know. No matter who answers the phone, talk to them like a friend. Usually I go straight through to the MD's secretary, so I say: 'Look, I'm sorry to interrupt you. But we offer sales training solutions for companies like yours. Who's the person I need to speak to in your company?' And nine times out of ten, they'll tell you. When I get through to the buyer, I say: 'I've just been speaking to Fred, your PA, and he told me you might be the person I need to speak to about this. I've got no idea whether or not you'd be interested, but what I'd like is to have a chat with you if I may.' Remember, your intention isn't to sell. It's to see if there's scope for both of you to work together.

Ready to Go?

Selling over the telephone is really exciting. You're literally seconds away from speaking to someone and trying out your sales skills. But before you start, you need to be prepared. You need to be really clear about why you're calling, know as much as you can about your customer and have your opening line ready to go. Before each and every call, you should go over the following pre-call checklist:

PRE-CALL CHECKLIST
What do you hope to gain from the call?
1.   Ideal outcome (sales order, sales appointment etc.) ❏

2. Fallback outcome (information about buyer or
    company, agreement for call back etc.)   ❏

Company information   ❏

Relationship history between you and your buyer   ❏

Your chat-up line   ❏

Your opening line   ❏

DOING IT: Sit by your telephone, take a few deep breaths
and try to imagine the perfect telephone call with a buyer.
You know the sort of thing: you ring, offer your chat-up line
and your buyer says: 'Great! That sounds perfect – exactly
what we're looking for. Tell me more...' Now pick up the
telephone, ring one of the potential buyers you researched
in Chapter 6 and give meta-selling a go.

13

REPEC for Brilliant
Face-to-Face Selling

What Buyers Won't Tell You – Picking up on Visual Clues

A great way to meet buyers is to arrange sales appointments, which means you'll be going out and visiting them in their office or place of business. Often, making face-to-face sales appointments is the primary goal of sellers when they contact buyers over the telephone, as meeting people in person can be a more successful way of closing business. You can take longer to build rapport during a face-to-face appointment, and there's more time to really find out about your buyer and ask for the business there and then. If you really love meeting people face to face, you can make sales appointments the primary goal of your telephone calls to buyers too. It really depends on you and the industry you're working in. Some products – especially very expensive products – are easier to sell face to face where you've got more time to establish trust with your buyer. Depending on what you're selling, you can also just go out and visit businesses speculatively, or talk to potential buyers at networking events. Use your own instincts about when and where to sell face to face, because it's not appropriate everywhere. Having said that, one of our meta-trainees has even sold in the pub.

CLAIRE: The first thing I do when I'm selling is go to the nearest pub – but not for the reasons you might be thinking! I sell discounted gas to bars, pubs and restaurants, so I simply walk into a venue and ask to speak to the manager. If I go in during the day when they're not busy, people are always happy to talk to me and it's a very successful way to make sales.

When you meet buyers face to face, the likelihood is you'll be visiting them for a previously arranged sales appointment in their place of business – essentially, their territory. As a seller, a buyer's territory is a rich source of information about the currency they're trading in, their values and goals. Everything about their place of business, from the pictures on the walls to the finish of the furnishings, should help you work out exactly what that company might need from your product.

DAVID: While I was selling for my old publishing company in London, we won the rights to produce the JRR Tolkien posters for 'Lord of the Rings' – and they were the only images ever approved by JRR Tolkien himself. 'Lord of the Rings' was massive at the time, the early 1970s, and incredibly popular with students. It was a real part of the drug culture, and I knew these posters would sell brilliantly at universities. So I visited Cardiff University bookshop in person and got chatting with the buyer. I could see a lot of posters already on sale rolled up in bins around the shop, so I knew I had to really position my product as something exclusive. I showed the buyer a dozen different posters and said, 'You can only have six of each of these.' Six of each design was a big order for me – six hundred quids' worth, and that was more years ago than I care to remember. It meant a real big thump in my commission for that month, anyway.

The guy, I remember, threw his pen down and swore at me, 'That's no bloody good, is it? Six of each – they'll be gone in a day.'

So I said, 'How many do you want then?' So he said, 'We'll need at least a hundred of each.'

I was in a real tight spot. He'd just asked for a hundred, and I'd only offered him six of each. So I said to him, 'Let me just go and make a phone call.' I went outside and walked around the block, wondering how I was going to get out of this one. But then I had a brainwave, so I came back and said to him, 'Look, I've spoken to the guys from dispatch. They've OK'd it for you to have twenty of each because you're such a good customer, and we're going to put five orders through of each so you'll get your hundred.'

That was more commission than I'd ever made before, and I doubt I would have positioned my product so well if I hadn't met the buyer in person and had a chance to pick up visual clues about the business.

Often you'll be lucky enough to meet a buyer in their personal office, so you'll have a real insight into their values as an individual. This can be exceptionally useful for building rapport. People tend to scatter their personal work territory with trophies to let you know what they value, so you'll have real insider information which will help you get on your buyer's wavelength.

DOING IT: Think about a place of business you've visited recently – perhaps for a job interview, work or meeting a friend. Write down five things you noticed about the décor, furnishings, office layout etc. that pointed towards the values of that organisation. Perhaps the desks were all arranged so everyone could talk to each other, suggesting a friendly, social workplace. Or maybe there were lots of recycling facilities because the company really values community responsibility. Make a note here of what you saw, and what you feel it tells you about that organisation:

14

After the Sale – Negotiating a Great Deal

What Negotiation Isn't

Negotiation isn't selling. It's the discussion over price or the terms of a sale that sometimes takes place *after* the sale has been agreed. If you were dating, negotiating takes place when you're already in a relationship. The exciting first evenings out are over, your best outfit is on the bedroom floor and your date is in the kitchen helping themselves to coffee.

Selling is where you help a buyer to buy. Usually, this means your need to sell is greater than the buyer's need to buy – at least at first. Your aim as a seller is to find out what your buyer needs so you can build desire for your product. Negotiation happens on a much more even footing. The buyer has already agreed to make a purchase, and now you're just settling the terms in a way that makes everyone happy.

Sales virgins often fall into the habit of negotiating too early in a sale – and sometimes negotiating when they really don't need to. You don't always need to negotiate, and in fact ideally you shouldn't negotiate unless absolutely necessary. Here are the four 'don'ts' of negotiation:

1. Don't negotiate until you've gone through REPEC and won commitment from your buyer.
2. Don't negotiate unless absolutely necessary.
3. Don't concede. It's OK to give way over something, but you should get back something else in return – i.e. exchange a price discount for a signed order form.
4. Remember you and your buyer are equals, so don't feel under pressure to give in to a buyer's demands.

The last point is really important: when you negotiate you and your buyer are equals. You're two consenting adults who've agreed to the sale, so – as long as you're not negotiating too early – you won't lose the sale if you don't give the buyer exactly what they're asking for.

Pleasing Everybody: The Art of Give and Take

Why negotiate? If the buyer is eager to buy, surely you could just firmly stick to your original terms of the sale and that's that. Well, that's true – but what about making sure your buyer feels good after a sale? What about your long-term relationship with them? You negotiate to make sure your buyer feels good, but you're under no obligation to give in if they're asking for something unreasonable. The real art of negotiation is this:

Make your client feel as though they've won.

First and foremost, just like selling, you should go into negotiation prepared. You'll feel much more comfortable if you know your moves in advance.

DOING IT: So now you're going to plan for negotiation. Answering the following questions will make sure you're fully prepared:

1.   What can you trade and what can't you trade? Can you drop the price or throw in extras – or both? Is there anything you can offer that costs you nothing, but makes the buyer feel they're getting added value? Make a list of all the possible variables before you start. The longer your list, the more flexibility you have.

2.   What's your favourite position? No, not that one. What price can you offer a buyer that leaves you in your favourite position: one that keeps the buyer happy, but you still with a comfortable commission? This means you need to prepare your *top* price (an ideal one); your *middle* price (the one that is realistic) and your *lowest* price.

TOP £
MIDDLE £
BOTTOM £

3.   What price can you absolutely not fall below?

£

4.   Are you sure you want to negotiate? Consider your alternative to this negotiation. For instance, is it the end of the month and you desperately need this deal? Can you afford to turn away a job role because you didn't negotiate the salary increase you wanted? Thinking about the alternative will ensure you have thought about this deal properly.

LUCY: You should always aim high when you negotiate. It's been proven that the higher the aspiration of the negotiator, the more successful the outcome. Which basically means, aim for the best outcome and you're much more likely to get it. You should also follow the 'give and get' rule. Because you and your buyer are equals, for everything you give, you should also get something in return. So if you offer your buyer a discount, ideally you should come to an arrangement where they perhaps purchase an extra product. Or if you throw in something extra for free, perhaps your buyer can help you out by signing there and then.

DAVID: It's a good idea to paint hypothetical scenarios for your buyer when you're negotiating, painting as vivid and attractive a picture as possible. A great way to do this is to start your offer with these simple words: 'What if...?' So perhaps you might say: 'What if this software is rushed to your office later today for free, so you'll have the entire new package running on your computer by 3 p.m.?'

Shut Up!

When you negotiate, you should keep everything simple, to the point and make sure you keep quiet at the right moment. What's the right moment? After you've painted a hypothetical picture for your client and set the offer on the table. We suggest you use the 'basis close' during negotiations, which means you say something like:

> 'Based on everything you've said you wanted, which includes the very latest edition, the price is...'

And then shut up. There's no need to get into a conflict or a battle. Remember, you'll want to do business with them again in the future.

Part III
How to Stay on Top

15

Taking Care of Yourself and Your Self-Esteem

Why Even the Best Sellers Give Up When They Shouldn't
The key characteristic of really brilliant sellers who break sales records and make masses of commission is their motivation to succeed. In fact, we're so sure of this that the meta-morphose catchphrase is *attitude, not aptitude*. We don't care how well you did in school, how many different career paths you've tried out or that you've never been any good at maths. None of your experiences before matters: your success as a seller comes down to your attitude. No matter what you've been told, you have it in you to be a fantastically successful seller. Let us give you the meta-morphose facts of life:

1. You can achieve sales success much more quickly than you may think.
2. You can be a fantastic seller regardless of your experiences in life.
3. Attitude is more important than aptitude.

Simply by reading this book you're demonstrating you have the right attitude to succeed. So you've already got the key asset of a sales superstar.

But you also need to *keep* that great motivated attitude, even when you make mistakes (which you will – but you should look at them as learning opportunities), it's raining outside and a buyer who was just on the verge of committing suddenly quits their company and moves overseas. It's easy to be motivated in the beginning. But selling comes with its tough times, and it's equally easy to have your confidence shaken by a few bad sales calls and feel like giving up entirely.

DAVID: Unfortunately, it's part of our culture to bring people down if they get too good. When Tony Blair stood down and made way for Gordon Brown, you just knew the papers would be full of negative stuff about Brown before he even got into Number Ten. And they were. If you stand out too much, someone's going to try to hit you with a brick. But remember, if someone is trying to knock you down, it's probably because you're doing something right.

We've met sellers who've sold brilliantly for months and months and smashed all their company targets, only to lose confidence when a few sales don't go the right way. Once you're in the mindset of failure, nothing seems to go right. So you think to yourself, 'What's the point in trying?' The sad thing is, we've seen so many people with great potential give up just as the going gets tough. If only they knew that if they just kept going they could carry on their successes and win even more.

Our philosophy at meta-morphose is that what you believe will guide your behaviour, which will in turn affect what happens to you. We have a handy diagram to communicate this:

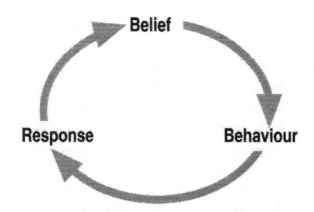

This isn't a new theory, but it's particularly relevant to sales. We've seen salespeople with great promise develop self-defeating beliefs after a few phone calls don't go their way. And as soon as they start believing nobody wants their product, what happens? They start using self-defeating language when they call customers. They're not enthusiastic or motivated, so they contact fewer customers and have fewer chances to make sales. As the sales targets begin to slip, they say to themselves, 'I *knew* I wasn't any good.' And so the cycle continues.

LUCY: It's vital you believe in your own success, even when things aren't going perfectly. You need to make sure a bad phone call or sales appointment doesn't affect your belief in your product or your ability to sell. It was just a bad call - that's it. Put it down to experience and carry on with the job.

The cycle of belief, behaviour, response is what's known as a self-fulfilling prophecy. If you believe something, you'll behave in a way that confirms it – and so what you believe happens. If you believe you'll fail, your confidence will go and you won't succeed. The trouble is, selling can be a bit like speed dating. It's great fun, but sometimes if you're talking to a lot of people and none of them is right for you it's easy to lose heart. If quite a few buyers aren't willing to commit one day and you're in the wrong frame of mind, you might feel as though you don't want to try again.

One of the things that will really keep you motivated is sales targets, and we're going to talk about that later on. However, just as important for your confidence is feeling that you *can* succeed – even if the last appointment didn't go well. Behind every motivated, confident, go-getting seller is a healthy bedrock of self-belief, and this is what you need to work at throughout your sales career. The good news is, self-fulfilling prophecies work the other way around too. If you believe buyers will respond well to you, more than likely they will. If you approach a buyer with the positive energy of confidence, they're more likely to trust you and listen to what you have to say.

DAVID: At meta-morphose we feel it's really important to build up the confidence of our trainees. Early experiences of education can really let down a lot of young people, and certainly not help them develop the right attitude to succeed in life. I've heard teachers telling kids that they'll never amount to anything. In my opinion, the education system can make a lot of people feel like real failures, so we try to put a good, healthy antidote to this in our training. There must be some good teachers out there, and I'm sure some inspire people to succeed. But mostly we find education doesn't offer strategies to deal with life when it doesn't go the right way. Most of us have learned to be hard on ourselves if something goes wrong. But this doesn't help us succeed.

So let's work on your confidence right now. First off, we should tell you you've got a great head start when it comes to being a confident seller. Because you've learned the *right* way to sell, you'll approach the sales situation with much more confidence than most new sellers. Not only have you learned the nuts and bolts of how to sell, you're also working with a philosophy that makes you feel like a good person. You're not approaching people to try to trick them or coerce them into buying. And you now know techniques it's taken us decades to learn. But in addition to that, you need to feel inside that you can sell, no matter what. Let's give you an exercise right now to get you feeling confident.

DOING IT: It's time to remember how amazing you are. We want you to think about five of your greatest achievements to date. Of course, there are even better achievements to come in the future, but for now focus on what you've done already. It really can be anything you've felt good about accomplishing – giving up smoking, travelling abroad, learning to drive... anything. Write them down here:

Now go back to the moments those achievements came true for you and try to relive everything: what you saw, felt and heard. The idea is to make you feel really good, and if something doesn't go right when you're selling you should go back and relive the times you did feel successful. This *really* works, by the way. Pretty soon you'll have even more achievements to add to your list.

If you're feeling unsure about your sales ability, or that selling isn't going the way you want, you can also focus on:

1. How much you've learned and how far you've come since you picked up this book.
2. The people you've made feel good by being interested in them and their business.
3. All the future sales that will make you feel brilliant.

You might have your own strategies for boosting yourself up when you're not feeling very successful – feel free to use them. This is your journey, after all.

Serious Commitment

It's important to remind yourself of your successes when you're not getting the results you'd like. But it's also important to put 'failures' into perspective. We've already explained that a buyer saying 'no' isn't really a rejection, and nor is it a failure. You've got vital information to use in the future, and you're one step closer to talking to someone who'll say 'yes'. Too many sellers base their self-esteem and self-image on meeting their day-to-day targets, which means they put a lot of pressure on themselves to get a 'yes' there and then from buyers. Now, targets *are* a very useful way to keep you motivated. And they can be a great confidence boost. In fact, we recommend you keep records of your finest achievements to remind you how brilliant you are – not just at sales but everything you do in life. But you shouldn't over-rely on getting great sales results to keep you feeling good, because then as soon as you get a 'no' you'll feel less confident.

At meta-morphose, we encourage sellers not to focus on each individual sales call or appointment, but on long-term relationships. You're not looking for one-night stands, but serious commitment. Therefore, don't base your success on what happens during one customer contact. In relationships, things aren't always smooth. Sometimes you have to compromise. Sometimes you have to wait. But you know in the long term your hard work will get you the right rewards

And finally, let's hear what a few of our meta-morphose sales team say about how to stay motivated and keep their confidence levels high even when the sales are down.

STUART: I've been selling for 25 years, so I've had my fair share of bad days. And if I don't feel selling is going well, what I say to myself is this: 'How I feel when I lose will determine how long it will be before I win.' If you're making cold calls, someone says 'no' and you stop to feel bad about it, you'll carry that feeling with you to the next call. And I've learned that's a great way to lose confidence. After all, if someone is going to say 'no', what's the point in trying? If, on the other hand, you don't stop to over-examine things, you'll feel good for your next call and you're much more likely to get a good result. That's why really good football managers make their teams focus on what they did well, rather than considering failure. The more a team concentrates on their successes, the better they're likely to play.

LISA: A really great way to keep your confidence up is through the support of other people. We've got a great sales team at meta-morphose, and I'm lucky enough to have other sellers around me who can cheer me up and keep me driven. If you don't work with people who help motivate you, your friends and family can help keep you feeling good even if things haven't gone as you would have liked.

Having said that, sometimes the day won't go your way and all you can do is go home, have a glass of wine and forget all about it - you can always try again tomorrow.

Why Experience Doesn't Always Count

Just because you're new to sales and don't have 'experience' doesn't mean you're at a disadvantage. Don't think people who've been selling for ten years will automatically be better than you – you can walk right into a sales situation with meta-selling and outperform the star seller within days. We're consistently amazed by just how well our meta-trainees do in the field, and the less you've been taught about sales already the easier you're likely to find the meta-morphose techniques.

Don't get us wrong: it's important to practise, and you will get better the more you sell. But don't think you can't compete with people who've been in the field longer.

DAVID: If you're new to selling, every moment you spend thinking 'Oh my God, the other sellers here are older than me, they know more than me, they have loads of experience and I don't' is a moment wasted. Knowing the right way to sell is much more important than experience in the field. We actually train harder at meta-morphose than in the sales game itself, and the exercises in this book are designed to give you experience of sales at its toughest. So you're already well prepared for any customer you come across - possibly more so than someone who's been selling for years.

The truth is, sales 'experience' can sometimes be a hindrance rather than a help. If sellers have been taught the wrong techniques they probably won't be as good as you, even if they've made thousands of sales calls and met hundreds of customers face to face.

> DAVID: Of the thousands of people we train, those with sales experience are always the most difficult to educate. The hardest job we have to do is retrain someone who's been trained by someone else in old-fashioned, unethical sales techniques. That's why at meta-morphose we usually approach graduates to join our training – because they're somewhat of a blank canvas, and less likely to have picked up the bad habits of many experienced sellers. If you're learning selling from scratch – and you're learning meta-selling – you have a fantastic advantage over the many sellers who've been taught the wrong way. Having said that, it is possible to retrain people who already have sales experience. If you've already worked in sales, you can learn the meta-morphose method as long as you don't mix and match it with other ideas you've learned and are fully committed to change.

Sales experience can also breed *assumption*, even in the most ethical sellers. What we mean by that is, even if a seller has been taught the right techniques, they can fall into the trap of assuming they know all about a customer before they've *listened*. This can be a hazard of meeting lots of customers – you meet someone similar to a previous buyer and assume their needs will be the same as someone you met before.

> DAVID: I've seen older salespeople – and I don't mean in age, but people who've been around a while – lock on to something a buyer clearly doesn't want and keep pushing it to them. And it's because previously they've met

a buyer who did really want whatever benefit they're flagging up, but the seller hasn't bothered to listen to what this buyer wants.

Just like experienced daters, experienced salespeople can think they know it all – leaving the game wide open for polite, interested meta-sellers to sweep buyers off their feet. We've met quite a few sellers who've been great at one time, but become victims of their own success and simply stopped listening to buyers. If they were on a date they'd be saying, 'I know *exactly* how you like your eggs in the morning.' And then they're flabbergasted when young, 'inexperienced' sellers somehow outperform them…

When you become experienced, don't *you* stop listening to your customers – no matter how similar they seem to someone you've sold to before. Don't get complacent and think you know what a buyer wants. Listen, listen, listen – we can't stress this enough.

Virgins Do It Best

Our meta-trainees have got some great results with hardly any experience at all – and certainly above and beyond what anyone might imagine a sales virgin to achieve. You've been trained in the same techniques. Which of these meta-sales star stories is likely to be yours during your first year of sales?

Within months of landing her first sales job with a pharmaceutical sales company, Claire exceeded her daily call targets so magnificently that company targets were changed to bring the rest of the team up to her standard.

In her first month as a seller for a franchising company, Catherine earned an entire year's salary. Within six months she was making £100,000 of sales per month and a very healthy commission indeed.

After less than a year as a salesperson, Hannah consistently outperforms a much more qualified and experienced colleague in the IT industry in which she works.

Gareth won almost £100,000 worth of business for his company during his first year of sales, earning a hefty commission and developing excellent relationships with several key customers.

At the end of his first year as a salesperson, Ben was top-selling account manager within a sales team that covered Northern England, Wales and Scotland – even though he was by far the youngest seller. Despite a tough year for his company in general, he also achieved 99.5% of his sales targets.

Oh Behave! Cures for Low Self-Esteem

So we've already told you that what you believe will affect your behaviour – which in turn will influence what happens to you. But now we're going to look at this in more detail, because it's vital you know just how important your beliefs are when it comes to selling. First of all, let's examine your beliefs about yourself.

DOING IT: Have a think about your beliefs. What do you think you're good at? What do you really struggle with? What do you really hate doing? The chances are, whatever you *believe* will already have come true for you. Think about a really strong belief you have about something you're *not* good at. Write it here:

Now write down the behaviours you do as a result of that belief:

Now write down what happens when you carry out those behaviours:

Can you see how your beliefs drive everything full circle, so that what happens to you is likely to reinforce any beliefs you have? But the belief is at the beginning of the circle: it's the thing that starts everything off.

LUCY: I always believed I couldn't draw. And even though I've been teaching trainees all about how belief drives behaviour, I didn't question this idea until recently. It suddenly occurred to me it was only my belief that I couldn't draw. And it was this that was the problem, not my ability. Whenever someone asked me to sketch something, I'd always avoid doing so. Or if I did, I'd apologise for it, saying, 'Really, I can't draw!' So I read a book that showed me how to, and I realised actually it's not as impossible as I thought. It showed me how drawing could be broken down into circles and shapes, and suddenly it all seemed so obvious. I can draw, as it turns out. It was only my belief that was holding me back.

New sellers often get 'beginner's luck' and do really well during their first day, week or month of selling – often better than veteran sellers on their team. Of course, this isn't beginner's luck. It's the belief new sellers have that selling is easy and there's no reason why buyers won't want to talk to them. But at one point they have one bad call or a sales appointment goes wrong, and suddenly they don't believe they're any good at selling – and a negative belief spiral comes into play. This is where negative behaviours resulting from a belief bring about exactly what you fear, and reinforce the negative belief that was at the beginning of everything.

> LUCY: I truly love cold calling. But if I were to believe that I didn't like calling new buyers, I'd behave in a totally different way. I'd be apologetic as soon as someone picked up the phone. And if someone told me they didn't take sales calls, I'd be so anxious to get off the phone I wouldn't start asking them nice, open questions about themselves. I won't make any progress, won't enjoy the call and my belief will be confirmed. However, if I believe that I have something of value to offer people and retain the spirit of curiosity, my behaviour will reflect this.

In sales, you'll speak to a lot of people and have many different experiences: good and bad. As a meta-seller we guarantee you'll have far more good experiences than bad ones, because you're an ethical and considerate salesperson. However, because you're speaking to so many people, the law of averages says a few of them will be having a bad day and won't want to talk to you.

DAVID: As a seller, you have to really believe that buy-ers will be interested and willing to talk to you, and this is often the real challenge for new sellers. In your first year of sales, you'll go through a whole spec-trum of emotions, from 'Good God, I'm a brilliant seller' to 'I'm terrible, why did I ever think I could do this?' At meta-morphose, we coach new sellers throughout their first year and most of this coaching involves re-gener-ating the right beliefs and getting people out of neg-ative spirals.

And not every sales appointment will go right. You'll make mistakes – especially in your first year of selling. But it's vital not to let a bad experience change your belief that you're a fantastic salesperson doing a great job. As a meta-seller, these are your beliefs:

- I'm a confident business professional.
- I have something important to discuss with buyers.
- Buyers are more than happy to speak to me.
  What I have to sell may not be right for some buyers and that's OK. There are other people out there who will be interested.

You can't start believing negative things because as soon as you do, you'll start behaving in a way that confirms this belief.

Instant Sex Appeal
How do you carry on believing in yourself, no matter what? The confidence exercises you've seen so far will help. And understanding that it's really your beliefs that determine what happens to you will help as well. But we've also got a

really useful technique for breaking down negative belief spirals and overcoming bad experiences in sales. Quite simply, you pretend you're someone else. At meta-morphose, we believe your mind is an incredibly powerful tool in determining your sales successes. If you're not feeling confident today, who do you know who *is* really confident and sexy? This can be the star seller on your team, a celebrity or even just an idea of a person who has the beliefs you want to emulate. Now simply pretend you're that person and voilà: instant confidence and sex appeal.

DOING IT: How do you pretend you're someone else? Easy. Picture the person in your mind down to the tiniest detail. Here are a few questions to help you:

How do they usually stand or sit?
What are they wearing?
How do they sound when they talk?
What hand gestures do they use?

Imagine you look and sound exactly like the person you're thinking of and really get under their skin. You'll find you start behaving differently too. Now phone up the second potential buyer you researched for yourself in Part I. Imagine the whole time you're someone else, and notice how confident this makes you feel and what great responses you get as a result. You might need to pretend you're a few different people before you find one that really works for you. If you like, make a note of some potential people here:

When you imagine you're somebody else, you behave in a different way. Those behaviours will change the responses you get, and this will have a big impact on your beliefs. You can be really creative with this role-playing technique and pretend to be absolutely anyone who is achieving what you'd like to achieve. For example, you might want to pretend you're a champion seller who's won loads of awards and makes record-breaking commission every month. Or perhaps you're someone who's totally addicted to cold calling. You can't keep away from the phone and you love finding out about people on the other end of the line.

DAVID: Have you heard the old joke about how many psychologists does it take to change a light bulb? The punch line is: one, but the light bulb really has to want to change. I don't want to get too much into psychology, but it's true that you really have to want to change your beliefs if you're to succeed in changing your behaviour. We can show you what works, but you have to be the one to put it into action.

Be Your Own Sales Coach

After our meta-sellers learn REPEC and begin working in sales, our coaches are only a phone call away to make sure they keep their confidence up and avoid a negative belief spiral. With this book, you have in your hands your very own meta-morphose coach – not for a year, but for life. Whenever something isn't going right, you can simply refer back to REPEC, go over the confidence exercises in this section and read advice from the meta-morphose team. But you can also be your own sales coach. It's important to be able to boost yourself if things aren't going well and a good way to do this is to have some sort of motivational message you can call upon. Here are some examples of what the meta-morphose team say to trainees – and themselves – to keep them motivated and successful.

- Follow the ten B4 ten rule: make ten cold calls before 10 a.m. This will get your energy levels up and make the day work for you in the right way.
- Enjoy the good times and look through the bad times.
- You must always push the limits of what you can do, because if you never fail you can never really succeed.
- Fortune favours the bold.
- It's better to try and fail than not try and always wonder 'What if…?'
- Strong lives are motivated by dynamic purposes.
- Welcome trips outside your comfort zone. If you have to call up an industry you've never dealt with before, this is a brilliant opportunity to expand your horizons and with every step outside the comfort zone your landscape will grow – and so will your confidence and achievements.
- Every day do the thing you're most afraid of first. The rest of the day will be easy.
- If someone tells you straight up they can't buy what you're selling, they've done you a massive favour. They've given you more time to find other buyers.
- Courage is the first of human qualities, because it's the quality that guarantees all others.
- Sales is all about courage: the courage to ask the question and more importantly to carry on asking the question.

DOING IT: You can use the meta-morphose team's motiva-tional statements to give you a boost when you need it, but why not find your own? Is there a saying that really moves you and makes you want to succeed? If not, do a bit of research and see if you can find something that really gets you going. Write your personal motivational statement here:

Getting into Bed with Your Buyer

When you're new to sales, and sometimes even when you've been selling for an awfully long time, you might not 'click' with a buyer, despite your best efforts. In those situations, we've got a great technique for really getting under your buyer's skin and working out what they want from you. We call it the 'memory process', and it's basically about going back into the memory of the selling situation to find out more about your buyer – from your buyer's point of view. It works much better for face-to-face selling situations because you've got much more material (visual, audio and kinaesthetic) to try to re-evoke the memory. However, you can try it for phone selling too. This technique is something you use *after* you've been in a selling situation, and the idea is once you've seen things from the buyer's point of view, you can go back to them and try the sale again.

> DOING IT: Imagine you're back in the sales situation. Remember the temperature, if there were any strong smells around, the details of your surroundings and where you and your buyer sat or stood. Notice what your buyer was wearing. Did they have any jewellery? How about a watch? Did they have their hair styled, or use any unusual hand gestures?

Now imagine you're the buyer. Imagine you're sitting where they sat, or standing where they stood, and look down at your hands. What's your skin tone like? Are you wearing rings? How are you holding yourself and feeling inside? Look over and see you as a salesperson selling to you as a buyer, and try to feel what your buyer must have felt at various parts of the sale.

This is a really effective technique for working out what your buyer really wants, and getting in touch with intuition that you didn't have time to listen to during a sale.

DAVID: I used the memory process technique on Lucy after one of her sales appointments hadn't gone well. Within seconds she'd worked out the buyer was someone who didn't like change – and yet before the presentation Lucy had been told the company wanted something really dynamic. So she'd arrived with an all-singing, all-dancing sales presentation, and here was a buyer who didn't want anything dynamic at all. Armed with this knowledge, Lucy could go back to the buyer and say: 'Look, I know we didn't get it right for you last time. Can we try again?'

16

Great Service Means More Success

How to Keep Your Customers

Intelligent sellers know that a sale isn't a one-night stand. It's just the beginning of a long and profitable sales relationship with your customer. And during this healthy, happy relationship, which has been built on total honesty and trust, you need to look after your customer – which means offering great customer service.

When you're selling to business – especially when you're selling expensive products – customer service is *really* vital to your long-term success. We've already explained that building trust with your buyer is an essential foundation of any sale. But you have to maintain that trust by making sure your buyer gets exactly what they want from your product and can talk to you easily if they have any questions or concerns after they've made a purchase. Our sellers at meta-morphose know customer care is an essential part of their role.

> TOMMY: I always try and imagine myself in the shoes of my client and wonder what I would want from my supplier after I've made a purchase. Each account needs to be handled differently: some need lots of love and attention all the time, some just need help when things aren't working.

If a customer doesn't feel looked after when they've made an expensive purchase, they're not going to deal with you again. And they're probably not going to recommend you either. Good sellers are brilliant at taking care of their existing customers after a purchase. This involves:

- Making sure customers get exactly what they've paid for.
- Ensuring buyers can easily get in touch if they have any questions or concerns.
- Keeping buyers up to date with product developments.
- Taking the legwork out of reordering by contacting customers ahead of schedule.

LUCY: I still remember with absolute clarity arriving in Crete around Easter time to find the apartment closed up, the pool empty, the bar shut until May and, to cap it all, it was pouring with rain! It's really important to deliver on your promises. If anything, your customers should feel they're getting slightly more than they expected, not less.

DOING IT: When you've closed a sale, how are you going to make sure your customer gets their product? Is there a delivery process? If you don't know already, find out exactly how you're going to cement the sales process by making sure your customer receives what they've paid for.

Call Me

You should make certain your buyers can contact you if they have any questions after they've purchased your product. Give customers your business card after you've made a sale and invite them to give you a ring any time if they have any questions. You might also want to send them a follow-up letter or email to welcome them to your product line and invite them once again to get in touch if they need to.

DAVID: Some companies send new customers welcome letters when they've made a purchase, saying 'Welcome to the club, glad to have you on board'. This is a great way to ensure customers have your contact details and feel truly taken care of. Good sellers go the extra mile to make customers feel good after a purchase. Not only is it the ethical way to behave, it also makes sure your customer is happy to order again from you in the future.

DOING IT: Time to get creative again. How are you going to make sure customers can contact you if they have any questions? Perhaps you'd like to call them from time to time to check everything is running smoothly. You could also send Christmas cards, or keep an eye on their company in the news and email them to congratulate or commiserate when something hits the headlines.

As well as making sure your buyers can get in touch, you can contact existing customers when you've got new products. Having already built up rapport and trust with your buyer, it should be quite straightforward to talk to them about product developments. Here's what one of our sellers at meta-morphose has to say about contacting customers after a sale.

MATTHEW: Always keep customers informed about new products and ask for their advice and recommendations. This is a great way to sell more products and show you care about your customer, whilst also gathering material to improve what you offer.

However, remember if you're contacting buyers to talk about new products, all the usual rules of meta-selling and REPEC apply. Research beforehand to make sure your product is relevant for your buyer, and listen to your customer before launching into a sales presentation.

If you're selling something that can be reordered or renewed, you need to keep excellent records of who might need what and when. There's really very little difference between customer service and selling. In fact, helping existing customers reorder existing products *is* selling. Repeat business is just as valuable as new business, so as a seller it's your job to look after customers already on your books. Make sure you've got all their details recorded, including the times they're likely to need reorders of your products. You should have some sort of system to remind you when to contact buyers for reordering. If you're lucky, wherever you're working will have a database to automatically bring up customer details when they need to be contacted for a possible reorder. But if not, you can record details on your email alarm system, mobile phone calendar or even a good old-fashioned pen and paper diary. If you phone customers in good time and make reordering as easy as possible for them, you'll be assured of a very easy sale and a buyer who feels totally taken care of.

DAVID: A few months before your contract is up with your mobile phone supplier, they'll ring you up and offer you a new phone. 'It'll be in your office tomorrow,' they tell you. And you think to yourself, 'What a brilliant company.' Of course, what's really happening is you're signing another 12-month contract with them. But you don't feel that way, because you're being helped to buy by a company that's already built up rapport and trust.

17

Scoring Keeps You Motivated

Why Goals and Scoring Are Important

In order to sell, you need to be motivated. And a really good way to motivate yourself is to have a goal or target: something you're excited about and will feel a real sense of satisfaction for achieving. Whenever people achieve something fantastic, you'll find they almost always had a goal in mind beforehand. Sports champions have records they want to break, managing directors have set amounts of annual turnover they want to achieve, and great sellers have monthly or weekly sales targets.

Most sales teams have shared sales targets, and that's great. Company sales goals can be a brilliant way to motivate yourself, especially because you get a good sense of what you're achieving compared to the other sellers around you. When you're the best, it's nice to know you're the best – and have it enshrined on the company target sheet. However, a goal that holds value for one person may not hold value for you. It's important to have goals that truly make you feel great when you've achieved them. When you keep score of your progress, you should feel you're doing really well.

> DOING IT: Write down five things you're really proud of achieving. Give each one a mark out of ten for how good it makes you feel – with ten being the highest.

❑
❑
❑

❑
❑
❑
❑
❑
❑
❑

You'll find the goals you're most proud of are the things you found most challenging. So if you want to win a big score for your achievements, aim high!

Whether you decide to make your own sales targets, or feel the company sales targets are enough of a challenge for you, it's important you write down your goals and have a practical plan of how you're going to achieve them.

The meta-morphose golden rule of goals is this:

You must be able to realistically see yourself achieving your goal.

This means your goal must be practical and the sort of thing you can look at written down and think, 'Yes, it's entirely possible I can do that.' Actually, we really believe you should write down your goals. It gives them dynamism and a 'real-istic' quality.

DOING IT: Write down the first sales goal you think of right here:

MY SALES GOAL

Now write down a sales goal you can achieve within the next month:

MY ONE-MONTH SALES GOAL

And the next three months?

MY THREE-MONTH SALES GOAL

Also, in order to see yourself achieving your goal, you should have:

- A practical plan for achieving what you want to achieve.
- A realistic timescale for reaching your target – in months, not years.

It's important you have an action plan for your goals, with practical and realistic steps to success. Let's say, for example, you have your eye on someone you'd like to go on a date with, and your goal is 'I'd like to go out with so-and-so by the end of the month'. You could have no plan, of course, and hope somehow or other things will work out. But you're much more likely to be successful if you decide to:

- Find out about your intended date's interests.
- Find out where they hang out socially, and make sure you're there too whenever you can be.
- Dream up a date you think they'd enjoy.
- Ask them out.

It's the same in sales. It's one thing to decide on making a certain amount of commission. But it's a much better thing to say: 'I know I achieve one sale for every ten calls I make. And I usually make twenty calls in a day. I know I can increase the number of calls I make, but I should also work on converting more people to buyers. How will I do that? Well, I can watch other sellers who have a better conversion rate and see what they do.'

> DOING IT: You're going to plan how to achieve your one-month goal right now. You need to think of four steps you're going to take in order to accomplish your target. And they have to be practical things. For example, if you won £200 of commission last month and want to achieve £600 this month, planning to turn up to work every day probably isn't going to cut it. If you can't think of actions to achieve your goal, think of people who are already accomplishing what you would like. What do they do? Now write down the four things you're going to do to meet your target:

Timing is important if you want to picture your goal clearly and get there successfully. Your goal should be achievable within a short timescale. If you're going to stay motivated you have to have an end in sight, and that means setting a goal you can achieve soon. And a goal that can be achieved in a few months is far more likely to be realistic and relevant to your life at this moment in time. If you say to yourself, 'I want to be a millionaire', realistically you know this is unlikely to happen any time soon. But if you say, 'I want to earn £300 by the end of the month, so I can buy myself a nice new mobile phone', this is much easier to visualise, plan for and achieve.

LUCY: Share your goal. Research shows that you are more likely to achieve a goal if it is written down and shared with others. But be a little careful who you share your goal with and check that they have your best intentions at heart before you take their advice. Remember, this is your goal.

DOING IT: Now you're going to create a personal action plan, signed by you and with a date to review what you've achieved. Choose your favourite of the three sales goals you've just written, and write it down here:

Now write the four steps you're going to take to achieve this goal:

Write down the date you're aiming to complete your goal by:

Sign your personal action plan:

Make a note of your goal-completion date in your diary, or whatever system you use for reminding you of important dates. You're going to look back at these pages on that day and review your progress. How well did the steps work? Did you discover any new steps you're likely to use in the future? What have you learned that will benefit you? Write about how the actions you took helped you get where you wanted to go:

18

It's Not That Bad!

Why Buyers Are Secretly Crazy About You

We've given you some great tools and techniques for keeping a positive outlook when you're selling. But just to make sure you're feeling really good about getting out there and making sales, you should know that buyers really are crazy about you. A lot of the time, buyers are trying to hunt down services just like yours. Think how happy they'll be when the right person calls at the right time with exactly what they've been looking for.

When you've been selling for a little while, it's easy to lose sight of just how useful you are for your potential and existing customers. You're letting hundreds, and hopefully even thousands, of people find out about a fantastic product – and using expert knowledge to tailor solutions for their needs. Selling is what makes the world go round, and without salespeople like you the world wouldn't work as well as it does.

> DOING IT: Think about companies who have been helped by your product. If you're selling something brand new, imagine how your product will be used and just how much time and money your customers will be saving. Now list five reasons why companies will be really keen to hear from you:

After a few months in sales, your buyers will start telling you just how useful your product has been for them, and how happy they are with what you've sold them. You can use these comments to build up a compliments bank for yourself, and refer back to it if you ever start feeling there are no new buyers out there.

COMPLIMENTS BANK

It's Not You, It's Me

Often, when customers don't buy things it's for a whole variety of reasons that have nothing to do with the seller. It's easy to blame yourself when you don't make a sale, but you should remember customers are complex people with many things going on in their lives. If you ever need a bit of a sales pick-me-up, take a little look at this list below. It contains some common, and not so common, reasons why businesses don't buy products – and none of them have anything to do with the seller.

Some reasons people don't buy:

- The company is much smaller than you thought and genuinely doesn't need a product of your calibre.
- The company has just tied up its annual budget in a very dubious marketing campaign that isn't delivering very good results at all. Its staff sincerely regret this spending

decision, but don't want to admit this is the reason their budget can't stretch to new investments.

- A company has restrictions on what it can spend during a difficult financial period and doesn't want to broadcast that it's having cash-flow problems.
- The person you're talking to is about to leave the company and work for a rival, and therefore has little interest in buying new services.
- The owner of the company uses a family member who offers the same service you do and feels obligated to carry on using them – even though they're not very good.
- The company is in the process of being bought out, and may operate in a totally different way in the near future so all buying decisions are on hold.
- The buyer is off on holiday tomorrow and hasn't the least bit of interest in anything other than the temperature in Spain or how many euros they can get to the pound.

Why the Competition Isn't Up to Much

OK, so there are competitors out there, but you've taken a good, hard look at them already and worked out exactly how your product is better. And the good news is, it probably isn't as competitive as you think anyway. Lots of people might offer what you do, but really good service and great value for money are thinner on the ground than you might imagine. Listen to what a few customers say about buying as they see it.

Considering all the sales calls we receive, we should be overwhelmed with quality goods and brilliant customer service. But the truth is we hold on to a lot of our suppliers because they're familiar – not because they're offering anything outstanding in terms of cost or quality. We trust them and we know they work. It's really a case of better the devil you know. If someone polite and trustworthy approached me and explained how we'd benefit from changing suppliers, convinced me everything would work and made sure the switch over was hassle free, I'd be more than happy to change.

I hate pushy sellers, and I'm sure I turn down some brilliant products because I don't like the manner of the salesperson. There's nothing worse than someone phoning up my company and asking to speak to someone who left ten years ago – then telling me how much I'm going to love their product without even finding out my name. Whatever happened to good manners?

At the moment, we need a new stationery supplier. The one we use delivers us the wrong product more often than the right product – and sometimes misses us off the delivery schedule altogether. But I haven't got around to finding a new one, and no one seems to have sought us out to offer us this service. If they did, I'd jump at the chance!

You'd think with so many ways to buy things these days, it would be easy to find reasonably priced products when you need them. But I've lost count of the number of times I've phoned around trying to find a particular item and been greeted by unanswered phones, answering machines, wrong numbers or even just nobody seeming to sell what I'm looking for! At the same time, I'm contacted by salespeople offering services it's quite clear my company couldn't possibly have any use for. We're a paper manufacturer – why would we want to buy paper? If only sellers would do a bit of research to find out what we might be looking for, we could meet somewhere in the middle and all save a lot of time.

Good suppliers are like gold dust. When I find a company who are attentive to my needs and deliver what they say they will, I hang onto them for dear life. But I don't come across them very often...

Epilogue

When We Were Virgins –
The meta-morphose Story

We saved this bit until last, because we didn't want you to feel you had to read all about us – unless you wanted to. But actually, meta-morphose is a pretty interesting organisation and we didn't happen overnight. We were virgins once too, and when we were learning we didn't have anything like a meta-morphose training course or this book to teach us.

> LUCY: When I started in sales I, like many new sellers, was expected to pick up experience on the job. It was only after I'd been selling for five years (and by that time I was managing a team of 12 people) that I managed to get on a sales training course and had that great 'Aha – so that's how you do it!' moment.

It's taken us many years of selling, consulting and working with sales teams and graduates to distil the unique meta-morphose philosophy and techniques into the straight-forward training programme we use with our trainees – and are communicating to you in this book. We've had to find out what works through trial, error and observation. Years of it. And by reading this book, you're really taking advantage of us – but that's OK. Learn from our experience and fast-track your way to the top of the sales team.

> DAVID: Many of the meta-morphose ideas came about whilst I worked as a consultant and observed sellers. Once I'd pinpointed the behaviours and attitudes that

led to sales success, I trained some young graduates in exactly those things - including soft skills like rapport - and put them on the sales team of a struggling company. These early meta-trainees worked so well that the fortunes of this company were turned around and the owners ended up selling it for around five times what they'd paid for it. It became pretty clear to me that I'd really found a winning formula. Now all I had to do was find a way to make this work commercially.

After this success, I was sitting with a bunch of mates, most of whom owned their own companies or were senior directors, and we started talking about what had happened with these trainees. One of the guys asked me if I could train some sellers for him. Then another said, 'If you train them, I'll take two.' And a third bloke said, 'I'll take three.' And so it spiralled, until I'd agreed to train a load of sellers all at the same time. A year later most of my trainees were still with the people I'd placed them with, so I got a whole chunk of money from a business angel and started training people in Holland and all over the place. The metamorphose concept was proven, and we've been growing ever since.

If we were to sum up how our sales training is different, we'd say we teach a combination of 'heart and head'. You have to use your feelings as well as good, logical sales steps if you're going to do well. Our techniques are all about helping sellers use their intuition and realise the way they relate to people is fundamental to sales success. But we also explain sales step by step, to make sure sellers have good signposts to follow and don't get lost along the way.

DAVID: meta-morphose is pretty unique in that we train people in soft skills. By soft skills, I mean the touchy-feely stuff like rapport and emotional bonding rather than things like spot welding or engineering. When I started training, no one was really training this sort of thing, and it took a lot of selling, observation and experimentation for me to realise that soft skills can be taught. I still believe you can't train attitude. You either want to do brilliantly or you don't. But people who want to succeed can be taught rapport, listening skills and so on.

Of course, meta-morphose isn't just a collection of ideas and selling techniques. We're a successful business enterprise in our own right. How do we work? On a very basic level, we're a training facility for sellers, teaching the unique skills you've learned in this book in a totally original way. We have a custom-built sales training centre ready and waiting for any-one who needs it, and we train a mixture of new sellers and corporate sales teams. Our classrooms are really like no oth-ers, and our trainees are in for a few surprises during their training. Before the week is up, we get our trainees selling to 'real-life' buyers – in the form of professionally trained actors briefed to give them a hard time. No trainee leaves the meta-morphose facility without being totally ready for any sales situation, and although the training is hard work, most of our sellers tell us what they've learned is invaluable.

DAVID: At meta-morphose we basically do what big compa-nies have done for years, which is to take groups of peo-ple and train them in sales. The difference is, we do it at our training facility, which means any company, large or small, can afford to have their sales teams professionally trained. And of course, we inject our sales training with the unique meta-morphose philosophies and techniques, which show our trainees not only the fundamentals of sales, but also how to keep themselves confident and motivated in the long term.

So part of our business is training existing sales teams, and our techniques have been proven to double sales revenue for companies who invest in our services. However, the really unique thing about us is that we train 'sales virgins' whom we've identified as having great selling potential. We interview graduates every year to find those with the right attitude to succeed in sales. Incidentally, the reason we interview graduates is because universities are a good place to find young people of employment age all in the same place. It has nothing to do with education: it's attitude that's important to us, not aptitude.

Once our trainees are up to the meta-morphose standard, we match their interests and experiences with companies requiring sellers – much as a recruitment agency would do, but in a much more bespoke way. It's important our sellers are interested in the industry they're working for, and we say the same for you too: if you're not bothered about what you're selling, you won't be a great salesperson.

LUCY: It's pretty unusual for sales virgins to receive expert training. They may receive a day or two here and there from a senior member of the sales team, but by and large they're left to go it alone. So the people who really need encouragement, reassurance and advice are left without – usually at just the time they need it. Unsurprisingly, a lot of sellers quit before they've finished their first year and swear sales isn't for them.

During their first year in sales, we also offer one-to-one coaching for our new meta-trainees. After all, when virgins start a career in sales they often have all sorts of questions – not only about selling but about the working culture, office politics and so on. We provide our trainees with a hug if they need it, advice if it's necessary and a kick up the backside if that's what we think will help. We also bring them back into our training facility for a few more weeks during those 12 months to brush up on sales skills and learn a few new ones.

Because of the way they're taught and the one-to-one coaching they receive, the sellers we find and train are much more likely to get through the shaky first year in sales, when emotions and self-esteem can be all over the place. Just like any relationship, the first year of selling is full of passion and excitement, but also uncertainty and hard work. Our training makes sure sellers are prepared for this, and also have someone to talk to if they need it.

And this is why the meta-sellers we source and train are so successful: they stay with the same company for the long term. When a seller joins a company, it's usually not until year two that the best sales results come through – because by that time a salesperson has really found their feet and got to know the values and nuances of their organisation. So by year two, companies find they've got a seller handpicked for their industry, selling like a pro and on a lower basic wage than an 'experienced' salesperson.

Unlike other recruitment solutions, 93% of our meta-trainees are still with their placement company after the first year of sales, which is an outstanding statistic. Sales staff hired through recruitment agencies have around a 20% chance of still being with a company after a year – which means that 80% of salespeople hired this way are a poor investment.

DAVID: We make sure companies are well aware that by hiring meta-morphose trainees they're making a very sound investment in their future sales force. And we won't compromise what we offer and say, 'You can have this bit, and forget about this bit. How about we find you a trainee, but we'll cut the price for you by not offering coaching...' We won't do that because we know it will affect the results we get for our clients.

So that's a little about us, how we work and why we work. But really this book is all about you, and how you can sell. We hope you're really exciting about selling the meta-morphose way. We're certainly looking forward to your sales successes, and we hope you get a lot of useful advice and support from this book over the months and years of your sales career. There's really only one thing left to say now, which is this:

'Get out there, and get selling!'

If you would like to know more about the services meta-morphose International provides to clients, or opportunities in the world of business-to-business selling as a career, go to www.meta-morphose.co.uk or telephone 0800 120200.

E-mails

David Baker:
bakersbarn@aol.com

Lucy Ryan:
lucy@mindspring.uk.com